THE
PARANORMAL
CAUGHT ON FILM

Paranormal

D&C
David and Charles

THE
PARANORMAL
CAUGHT ON FILM

AMAZING PHOTOGRAPHS OF GHOSTS, POLTERGEISTS
AND OTHER STRANGE PHENOMENA

DR MELVYN WILLIN

A DAVID & CHARLES BOOK
Copyright © David & Charles Limited 2008

David & Charles is an F+W Publications Inc. company
4700 East Galbraith Road
Cincinnati, OH 45236

First published in the UK in 2008
First published in the US in 2008

Text © Melvyn Willin, 2008
Photography © see picture credits (page 140)

Melvyn Willin has asserted his right to be identified as author
of this work in accordance with the Copyright, Designs and
Patents Act, 1988.

A catalogue record for this book is available from the British
Library.

ISBN-13: 978-0-7153-2980-1 hardback
ISBN-10: 0-7153-2980-4 hardback

Printed in Singapore by KHL Printing Co Pte Ltd
for David & Charles
Brunel House, Newton Abbot, Devon

Commissioning Editor: Neil Baber
Editorial Manager: Emily Pitcher
Assistant Editor: Sarah Wedlake
Art Editors: Sarah Clark & Martin Smith
Designer: Joanna Ley
Copy Editor: Caroline Taggart
Editor: Verity Muir
Picture Researcher: Sarah Smithies
Production Controller: Kelly Smith

Visit our website at www.davidandcharles.co.uk

David & Charles books are available from all good bookshops;
alternatively you can contact our Orderline on 0870 9908222
or write to us at FREEPOST EX2 110, D&C Direct, Newton
Abbot, TQ12 4ZZ (no stamp required UK only); US customers
call 800-289-0963 and Canadian customers call 800-840-5220.

The Paranormal Caught on Film

Contents

Foreword

The camera cannot lie, it is sometimes claimed – wrongly. It can not only lie, but also deceive us in a number of ways, as any special effects expert can prove. When something appears on a photograph that by rights shouldn't be there, we have a choice of at least six possible explanations: it is (1) an outright fake; (2) an accidental (or deliberate) double exposure; (3) an example of 'photographer blindness', or failing, (as your eye is glued to the viewfinder) to notice the person walking across your field of vision, leaving a splendid ghostly trail on your print; (4) the camera strap straying in front of the lens, converted by the flash into what we imagine ectoplasm to look like; (5) a simulacrum, or natural object such as a cloud, tree or rock that can be seen as resembling a human figure, and finally (6) a genuine anomaly, an effect for which no normal cause can be identified. In *Ghosts Caught on Film* (David & Charles, 2007) Dr Melvyn Willin, Honorary Archivist of the Society for Psychical Research, assembled a splendid collection of strange pictures old and new that included, I suspect, examples of each of the above six categories. I am delighted to see that with this book he has done it again.

Deciding to which category a picture belongs can be difficult. Too often, especially with old ones, we do not know enough about the photographer, camera, film or scene being photographed to make a fair judgment. Can we be certain, for instance, that nobody walked across the church aisle while a time exposure was being made? That a leaf or plastic bag did not float past the lens as the shutter clicked? Or that the photographer forgot to get the thumb-strap out of the way? It is extraordinary how many of them do. However, when the photographer is still alive, apparently sane, and happy to cooperate with investigators, the choice of category becomes easier. Several of the pictures in this book were taken by amateurs who sent their prints to the Society for Psychical Research because they were genuinely baffled and sought an expert opinion, neither requesting nor receiving payment or publicity. Many of these were carefully examined by two well qualified experts, the late Dr Vernon Harrison, Principal Scientist with Thomas de la Rue and specialist in forgery detection, and Maurice Grosse, who questioned the photographers at length and was usually satisfied that their enquiries were in good faith.

'The diligent hen will find the golden kernel in the rotting dunghill' said Kepler, and Dr Willin is the most diligent of archivists. He suggests likely explanations whenever they seem appropriate, and when he cannot find one he is not ashamed to admit it. I found several golden kernels here and I am confident that the diligent reader will do the same. Cameras, I repeat, can lie. Yet they can also reveal some surprising truths and offer us tantalising glimpses of phenomena that we are obliged to label 'paranormal' simply because we cannot yet explain them.

Guy Lyon Playfair

Introduction

Welcome to the world of the extremely weird. This used to be called the 'supernatural', but the implication that unexplained phenomena were *above* nature rather than *within* it caused some problems, so people now tend to call it the 'paranormal' or beside the normal. I'm not too keen on that term either, since I would like to think that at least some of the phenomena within its remit are not paranormal at all, and that once explained they will become normal. 'Parapsychology' and 'experimental psychology' are too narrow to describe much of what is here and even 'psychical research' excludes some very interesting anomalies. So perhaps I should stay with 'extremely weird'!

This book follows on from my previous one, *Ghosts Caught on Film*, but this time not only examining more photographs of so-called ghosts, but also investigating other paranormal phenomena that people believe they have captured on film. Like *Ghosts*, it is divided into chapters devoted to phenomena that are linked in various ways. Choosing which images to place in which chapter was a difficult task since some have attributes that belong to more than one section, so you may disagree with some of my decisions. All I can say in response is that I have tried to be as objective as possible and have done my best not to sensationalize the subject or the material: that happens often enough in some areas of the media. But I'm sure I haven't always got everything right!

The first chapter, 'Ghostly Figures', contains some of the photos that we desperately wanted to put in the first book, but couldn't because of space limitations. Here you will find well-researched pictures that have often baffled the photographers; only rarely has someone jumped on the 'it must be a ghost' bandwagon. Many of the images from this and the last chapter in the book were sent to the Society for Psychical Research (SPR) in London, where they were scrutinized by experts and investigated in detail to assess their authenticity. It was important not only to make use of the skills of professional photographers, but also to understand the circumstances in which the shots were taken in an attempt to eliminate fraud and other factors. The meticulous records of the late Maurice Grosse, chairman of the Spontaneous Phenomena Committee of the SPR from 1977 until his death in 2006, were invaluable here; his collection also provided several examples of anomalous photos.

The second chapter presents unaccountable lighting effects and possible apparitions. Of course, one could argue that apparitions and ghosts should be placed in the same category, but I have tried to separate them here by including photos of what some people have interpreted as angels or spiritual mists.

The third chapter I found a great deal of fun. Magazines such as *Fortean Times* regularly delight their readers with natural objects – trees, rocks, waterfalls and so on – that bear a bizarre resemblance to living or mythical things. I regret that my publisher would not let me present images such as Mother Teresa in a bun or Krishna's cousin Neminath in Philadelphia cream cheese, but the line had to be drawn somewhere! Although most of the time we can simply smile and enjoy the coincidences, there are those who believe that these manifestations have a more serious side and that divine messages may be being conveyed via the objects in question.

I find the fourth chapter quite disturbing since it includes images of poltergeists, bleeding statues, a stigmatist and one example of alleged spontaneous human combustion (SHC). Although it is easy to dismiss these phenomena as misguided at best and fraudulent at worst, the thoughtful researcher should try to discover exactly what is going on with these disquieting subjects. It is too easy to blame all poltergeist activity on pubescent girls or all signs of stigmata on gruesome self-inflictions. Similarly, statues seeming to bleed have a profound effect on believers throughout the world and even different branches of hard science disagree over the data concerning SHC.

The fifth chapter brings ghosts back into the picture again, but this time with a survival slant. This does not necessarily imply a purely spiritualistic concept of maintained contact. It also allows for the possibility that the energy – or soul, if you prefer – that is the essence of an individual may be able to survive in some way beyond physical death. Perhaps the hotly debated, both for and against, 'Stone Tape' theory originally encountered in a BBC play in 1972 should be given another airing here. Briefly, it argues that the substance of a building can trap and record highly charged events and then in some circumstances play them back like a spectral video player. This could be suggested as an explanation for ghosts seeming to be oblivious to living people: they might be in a different time perspective.

Throughout the book I try not to provide didactic answers to the questions that are put forward. There are two reasons for this. One is that the subject is so complicated that it would be impossible in a book of this size to explore in great depth the issues that are raised here. The implications of the paranormal touch many different disciplines. The obvious examples are parapsychology, psychology, sociology and theology, but I would expand that list to include all the so-called 'hard' sciences as well as the arts. The second reason is that I would not presume to tell anyone that I have the answers to all the imponderable questions that arise. One's knowledge grows according to one's experiences and learning. I used to be sceptical about poltergeists, for instance, but my attitude changed considerably when I witnessed an incident at first hand – and had it verified by another person present. It seems to me the height of arrogance to believe that at any time one has the answers to life's mysteries. In all realms of study new information sometimes confirms theories, sometimes expands them and sometimes destroys them. Let us all keep trying to unravel these enigmas.

The book is aimed at a wide audience. Some will find it somewhat 'heavy' at times and others will desire more depth and academic scrutiny. Hopefully everyone will find it thought-provoking and, whether it is used as a coffee-table adornment or the basis of further research, I trust that it will be enjoyed. Perhaps it will encourage you to explore your own photograph albums to see if you have any strange or inexplicable shots lurking there. Further to this, I do encourage you to arm yourself with a camera at all times – in these days of camera phones it is almost always possible to take a snapshot. The more photographic evidence we can acquire, the greater the database we will build up for finding those few elusive photographs of genuine paranormal phenomena.

GHOSTLY FIGURES

So what is a ghost and what are its characteristics? The answer to the first question is 'I don't know', but there is sufficient evidence (I don't use the word 'proof') to suggest a very wide range of characteristics.

It can be transparent or opaque.
It can be solid or cloudy.
It can be unaware of our presence or make contact.
It can manifest through all of our senses except taste.
It can be recognizable or unknown.
It may or may not be time- and/or place-orientated.
It may or may not appear at times of crisis.
It can be human, animal or even take the form of a mode of transport.
It can soothe us or occasionally frighten us.

That list is far from being conclusive, but I think we might agree that there are many different types of ghosts, just as there are many different types of living human experience of them and perhaps this is a clue to their nature. It may be that a ghostly emanation of any kind requires human contact to act as a catalyst to its existence. The folklorist Eric Maple believed that if people ceased to believe in ghosts, ghosts would no longer be able to function. The power of belief has a considerable effect on one's whole being, as can be seen in medical trials using placebo drugs that sometimes work as well as the real thing. Is it beyond the bounds of possibility that a strong enough belief might be able to conjure up sufficient energy to create a tangible presence? In the 1920s Alexandra David-Neel certainly believed that she created a mind form (tulpa) that had a tangible existence, was seen by other people and was difficult to dispose of. There have been other similar claims with veridical evidence to oppose the allegation of hallucination. Furthermore perhaps we are bound to have difficulties in capturing on film what is by its very nature beyond an obvious definition or essence. We can photograph what electricity can do and we can hear what radio waves can provide, but their palpability can be discerned only through other agents. If ghosts are an unknown form of energy, then to learn more about them we need to record and study them without either the closed minds of some scientists or the gullibility and sensationalism of some spirit seekers and 'ghostbusters'.

In this chapter you will find many British examples, as one would expect from this most haunted island, as well as several instances from elsewhere. The settings vary from churches and graveyards to a mirror and even a kitchen sink! Some are inside, some outside. The provenance also varies: in some instances there is good evidence from contactable people; in others the information we have about the image is vague and the people long gone. The photographs have been taken using a wide range of equipment from old cameras to new digital apparatus, including the ever-present mobile phone. Where film has been used it varies from colour of a reasonable quality to old black and white. Despite the advancement in photographic techniques, transferring images from the original into book form can cause a certain loss of clarity. The publishers have firmly resisted any temptation to enhance the photos in this book and I can assure the reader that some of the originals are even more startling than the reproductions presented here. This was brought home to me in a very forthright way during a recent visit to Hungary, when I tracked down the original photograph of the Karácsond Virgin Mary vision (discussed in *Ghosts Caught on Film*) and was amazed at how clear it was.

I hope you enjoy this chapter and that you show the photos to your friends and family. Hopefully they will disagree with your interpretation – and mine – and provide further insights into what is happening in these intriguing shots. You could even try to reproduce some of the effects yourself, which does not necessarily mean that the ones shown here were produced in the same way. If you find yourself at any of the locations, make sure you have a camera with you. Who knows, your photographs may be included in the next book!

The Headless Woman

'Mike' writes of this shot taken by his father on a visit to Edinburgh Castle in around the 1980s: Mike's mother and sister can be seen sitting on a cannon. He reports that the print was found by chance when they were 'cleaning up the house' after his mother's death. In fact the figure is not necessarily headless – the transparent nature of her form makes it possible that her head is lost in the shadow of the stonework. There is a possibility that the image was caused by a double exposure – intentional or otherwise. Another suggestion might be that a person was standing in shot and then moved away during the exposure to leave a ghostly effect. However, the shape and perspective seem wrong for that explanation; neither does the figure resemble a chemical stain in processing or a lighting anomaly. The clothing does not seem to be consistent with what other people in the shot are wearing. The sleeves appear to be 'puffed' and the figure may be wearing a long white tail coat or a full-length dress. We are left with a mystery – but no hard evidence of a 'headless Victorian woman'.

'The clothing does not seem to be consistent with what the other people in the shot are wearing'

Reaper at the Waterfall

This atmospheric photograph was sent to the website ghoststudy.com. The picture was accompanied by this note:

I'm not the person who actually took this picture. It was sent to me by a friend. This photo was captured in West Java in Indonesia at the bottom of Mount Gede. The people in this photo are high school students who held a camp on that mountain.

Despite the site operator appealing for anyone to provide evidence for or against its authenticiy, nothing else is known about this picture. It was suggested, however, that the figure might be part of the mountain's rock formation, since the texture was similar.

The image of the 'grim reaper' is popular in folklore and in the minds of people through films and the media generally. If one cannot accept that such a character actually exists, then another possibility might suggest that a thought form is being created here, but why it would occur in this form and on this occasion baffles me.

'If one cannot accept that such a character actually exists, then another possibility might suggest that a thought form is being created here'

Face in the Pulpit

From the archives of the Society for Psychical Research comes this baffling photograph seeming to show a male human face coming out of the stone. It was taken by Donald G MacKenzie in May 1928 in a church on the Scottish island of Iona. He claimed the church was empty at the time and that nobody to whom he showed the photo seemed to recognize the mystery person. Assuming he was telling the truth, this precludes the possibility of an accidental double exposure, since in that case he would surely have remembered the other person when he saw the developed photo, even if he had not really registered his presence at the time. Although a photo taken before the days of computer technology is less likely than a more recent one to have been faked, the disadvantage with something taken 80 years ago is that the people involved are generally no longer available to help with further investigation!

'He claim
church was
at the time ar
nobody to wh
showed the
seemed to rec
the mystery p

Skeleton in the Stones

Egremont Castle in Cumbria is in ruins and not occupied. On 28 September 1977 this photograph was taken using a Polaroid Swinger camera. What started life as a standard shot of the photographer's boyfriend changed dramatically when she noticed various strange impressions, especially the semblance of a figure to the left and behind the seated man. Is it a skeleton wearing an orange frock coat with a raised ghostly hand holding a wand of some sort or is it a curious rock formation? Tourist Information advises that Jefferson's history of Allerdale-above-Derwent (near this site) mentions that 'several skeletons have been found at various times', though we have no specific evidence to link that statement with this photograph.

The tradition of the skull or skeleton being frightening has a long heritage in many cultures. As far back as the second century the Greek essayist Plutarch wrote in *Moralia* of the skeleton being a reminder of mortality; even today the skull and crossbones are commonly recognized as the flag of pirates. The association with death has been maintained throughout all the arts up to and including contemporary times. In music one encounters the 'danse macabre' (for instance Saint-Saëns' version), inspired by the poem of Henri Cazalis, and Liszt's *Todentanz* or 'dance of death', inspired by Holbein's woodcuts. There are many examples in the film genre, notably in Walt Disney's *Fantasia*, the impressive skeleton warriors created by Ray Harryhausen in *Jason and the Argonauts* and much more recently in *Pirates of the Caribbean* starring Johnny Depp.

'she noticed ... the semblance of a figure to the left and behind the seated man'

Ghost in the Kitchen Sink

The details behind this curious photograph from 1992 are somewhat bizarre and involve places as far apart as Sheffield in Yorkshire and Tunisia in Africa. Researchers from the popular British television programme *Schofield's Quest* forwarded the picture and this accompanying letter to Maurice Grosse, an expert in photographic anomalies. He was equally puzzled by it:

My name is Walter Collins, aged 15. Please, please, please help me and my mum to solve this mystery. The photograph appeared in our holiday 'snaps' from a two week holiday in Tunisia in 1992. The film was used and taken out of the camera in Tunisia. The strange thing is that the picture is in our kitchen at home. Another spooky thing is that there are two negative images on the negative strips, but only one print. HELP! It cannot possibly be someone dressed up because the person would be standing in our sink! (The side would not take the weight!) It has puzzled us for two years! I hope you can help!

If the story told is true then this is a very strange image indeed. Perhaps a combination of faulty memory and a double exposure produced this shot, or perhaps there is something more mysterious happening.

'It cannot possibly be someone dressed up because the person would be standing in our sink!'

Extra Figure in the Fire Station

'there was nobody else in the station at that time, and this has been verified by all present'

We do not normally associate fire stations with paranormal phenomena and it therefore came as quite a surprise when Maurice Grosse was sent a complete set of photographs from the fire station at Market Deeping in Lincolnshire. Only the last shot showed the extra figure on the right inside the station doorway. The pictures were taken on 26 January 1986 from approximately 25m (80ft), with 5–6 second gaps between shots. Mr Adams of the fire service stated '…there was nobody else in the station at that time, and this has been verified by all present.'

I think one can discount either fraud, lighting effects or developing anomalies here, but the figure does appear to be very solid and I wonder whether it may be an extra person who accidentally came into view and whom the photographer had either forgotten about or not seen – photographer blindness. It might be an administrative worker, cleaner, friend or even a member of the public. The figure appears to be holding something in its right hand and wearing a white blouse or shirt – it has been suggested to me that it might have been a female worker with a handbag about to go off home. Despite interest from local and national television as well as the press, no reasonable answer has been found.

A Ghostly Prayer

The church in Eastry, near Sandwich in Kent, is dedicated to the Blessed Virgin Mary and is thought to date from the eleventh or twelfth century. The details for this photograph are scant. It is generally believed to have been taken by Mr Bootman (or Botman), a bank manager, in September 1956, when he was alone in the church except for a cleaning lady. Although the image is often referred to as a 'ghostly vicar' it is possible that lighting or the chemicals used in development 'created' the shadowy figure. This might then be an example of pareidolia; that is, twisting images around in one's mind to form a recognizable likeness. A double exposure would also produce a similar image.

Alan Murdie, ex-president of the Ghost Club, comments: 'I have come to the conclusion that apparitions cannot be photographed, although they might leave traces on film (fogs, smudges etc.) in the same way a fish may leave ripples on a pond – but the ripples are not the fish!' This viewpoint may be sceptical, but it still allows for the possibility of paranormal phenomena being caught on film. In this example, even if the image is not a ghost, a genuine unknown presence may still have caused the 'fogs, smudges etc.' to be manifested and photographed.

'the image is often referred to as a "ghostly vicar" '

Witch of the St Anne's Castle

Some 15 years ago I held a number of investigations at the St Anne's Castle public house in Great Leighs, near Chelmsford, Essex. The pub has a long history of haunting and poltergeist activity, as well as a direct link to witchcraft via the story of the 'witch of Scrapfaggot Green' and the boulder that was placed over her grave and subsequently moved by American forces during the Second World War. On the occasion when this shot was taken I was with a group of experienced investigators who were placed at different locations in and around the pub with recording apparatus. Rules concerning the movement of people were strictly adhered to in order to avoid misunderstandings, and nobody was alone, since verification is always necessary for any subsequent claims.

Late into the night a muffled sound was heard and my companion Jeff took two quick shots into the darkness. We saw nothing except the flash of the camera illuminating the adjacent room. At the end of the stake-out we met up to discuss what had happened and confirmed that nobody had left their posts nor witnessed anything strange, apart from the usual coldness and excitement at the possibility of capturing something paranormal. It seemed that the investigation had been a failure until the two photos were developed. One showed the empty room and the other clearly showed an unknown woman seemingly dressed in modern clothes. It is possible that photographer (and observer) blindness was to blame, but the woman did not match the description of anyone else present. Of course, it could have been an intruder, but this also seems unlikely.

'Nobody had ... witnessed anything strange, apart from the usual coldness and excitement at the possibility of capturing something paranormal'

The Casino Ghost

'The shape seemed
too clear to be dust
or smoke'

This picture is one of many interesting images collected by the website ghoststudy.com and, unusually, it is accompanied by some details of its provenance. We are told that 'Mark' took the shot of his girlfriend with a camera phone at a restaurant at the Burswood Casino in Perth, Australia, on 16 February 2005. About a month later friends started pointing out the strange shape behind the girl's head. The shape seemed too clear to be dust or smoke and a double exposure on such a camera is very unlikely, if not impossible. It was suggested that the image could be that of a lady in an orange dress or something similar, with strangely coloured face and hair, but nobody seems to know for sure. Mark remains sceptical, but he is open-minded enough to admit that it is 'freaky'. Did someone pop in and out of the shot or is it an example of an apparition?

The photo is unusual in that paranormal images are not often taken in restaurants. We are all aware of the graveyard syndrome or haunted houses and castles, especially in the UK, but to capture such an image in this setting is particularly welcome. Perhaps it is another example of places holding 'highly charged' memories that can be conducive to paranormal phenomena.

Face in the Mirror

There seems nothing particularly unusual about this image at first glance. It is a room containing historic furniture – a four-poster bed, tapestry curtains. It is in fact a room in the Halls Croft Building in Stratford – the house that once belonged to Shakespeare's son-in-law and dates from the early seventeenth century. A member of the Haunted Britain investigative team was visiting the house and took this photograph, only later discovering the figure reflected in the mirror. According to the photographer, there was no one else in the room. If you imagine where the reflected person must have been standing, if indeed there had been someone there, he would have been just in front of the photographer to the left and facing him. Hard to miss, one would have thought! Could it be the apparition of one of the house's former inhabitants? The figure appears to have a dark jacket and white shirt or possibly a lace cravat – popular wear for gentlemen in the seventeenth century.

If there really was no one else present in the room, it is certainly intriguing, but I have in the past used mirrors to produce contrived shots that looked very convincing. At a 'ghost hunt' in Scarborough in the 1970s I was offered money by a newspaper to allow them to print my fake Polaroid of a reflected skull-like face as a genuine ghost photo. I declined their offer.

'the house ... once belonged to Shakespeare's son-in-law and dates from the early seventeenth century'

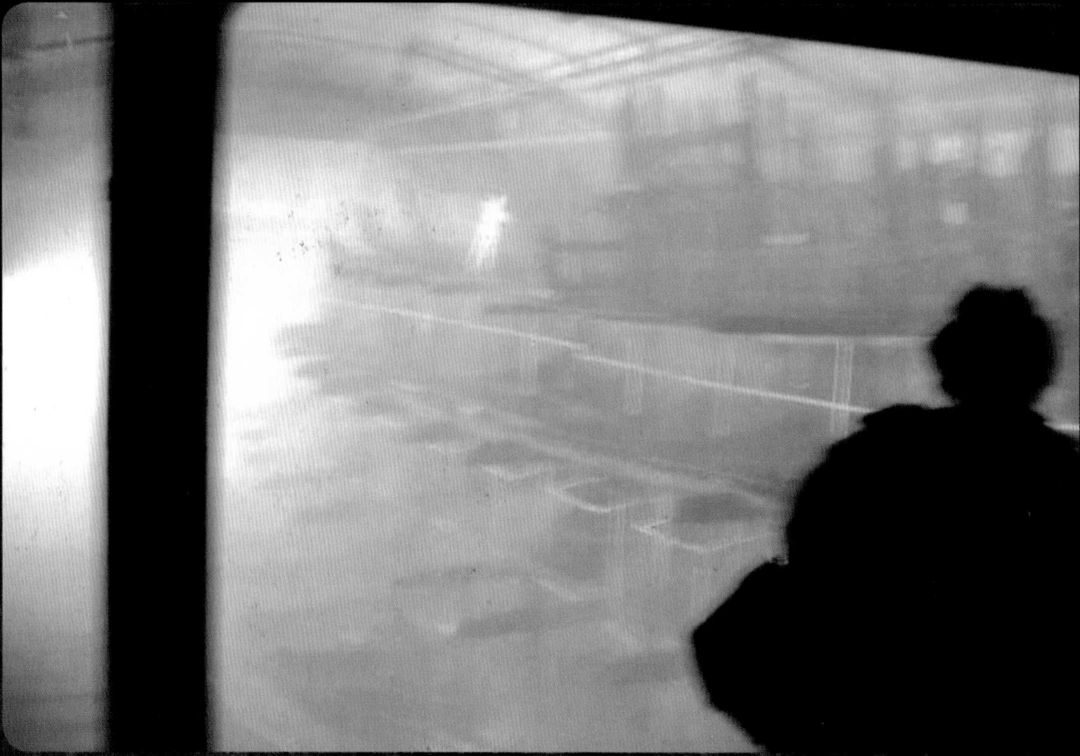

The Ghost of the *Mary Rose*

'There is no explanation for the white image that can be seen in the background'

This shot is both intriguing and frustrating. Dated 1995, it is part of the Maurice Grosse Collection held in the SPR Archive; although it is accompanied by a handwritten letter the details are inconclusive and the person named and the phone number given are no longer obtainable. What we do have is a photo 'taken from the Observation Gallery through a glass partition'. The person in shadow in the foreground would appear to be a lady carrying a bag over her left shoulder, standing in front of the exhibit of Henry VIII's flagship the *Mary Rose*. There is no explanation for the white image that can be seen in the background. Maurice Grosse obviously thought it worthy of further investigation, but his precise findings have not been discovered. The mystery remains.

The Ghostly Barmaid

In 1994 this photo was sent to the Society for Psychical Research by a Mr Smith of Sunderland, Tyne and Wear. He also provided the negative, which showed no sign of tampering, as well as details of the image, which are as follows:

The photo was taken 25–30 years ago in a pub in Whitley Bay, Newcastle upon Tyne. It was taken on an old type of film made by Agfa that has been out of production for many years… The bar had just been refitted and the owner asked me to take a photo of it. As you can see the lady appears to be moving out of the back of the bar with the room thermostat and part of the door surroundings through the front of her body and the back of her solid

If this is not a ghost then the most likely possibility is that a living figure was caught in the shot without the photographer noticing it. Alternatively the photo could have been taken fraudulently but the figure is somewhat blurred and one is tempted to suggest that if the photographer had inserted the image on purpose he or she would have made a better job of it.

'the lady appears to be moving out of the back of the bar'

35

STRANGE LIGHTS & APPARITIONS

'Strange lights and apparitions' – a title with two concepts and multiple interpretations, some separate and some entwined. The strange lights could be just that, which would have justified my including the aurora borealis (northern lights) or the light quality experienced during an eclipse. However, with the photos of lights shown here, there is an implication that something we don't understand is happening. That leads us into the possible world of the apparition – a notoriously loaded word and open to as many definitions as one can imagine. To cite just one example from this chapter, consider the photograph taken in Cyprus (see page 54): is it an apparition or simply a strange light? All the usual questions of verification and research can be asked of it, but one is still left with the same dilemma.

Within this chapter we also present a curious picture of what might be astral projection (see page 40). Sceptics will be horrified to read this, as may those who believe in the human soul, although the person photographed was not, as far as we know, having a near-death experience at the time. Do this and other light manifestations have a natural and simple explanation or are we discovering here something new and perhaps as controversial as an unknown energy field?

Probably the most contentious material in this chapter concerns the photographs of angels. The arguments attempting to refute the existence of angels are well known and I do not propose to go through them all here, but they include the fact that the wings of the stereotypical Renaissance angel are not big enough in relation to the body to enable lift-off unless the supernatural – yes, I mean 'supernatural' – is brought into play. Sceptics

also maintain that angels are either figments of our imagination or semi-deities introduced in various mythologies, and notably in Christianity, to act as messengers to us and adversaries to those nasty demons. Let us not forget that Lucifer was himself a fallen angel. The idea of guardian angels was given a huge impetus after Arthur Machen's short story 'The Bowmen' – relating how the beleaguered British army was saved from possible annihilation when angelic bowmen appeared in the sky and drove away the enemy – was treated as fact after the Battle of Mons in Belgium on 23 August 1914. In the best possible tradition, of course, the angels were on the side of the good and righteous, which on this occasion would seem to mean the British. In the true spirit of urban legend what happened next was that people started coming forward, for whatever reasons – genuine, misguided or corrupt – to tell their personal experiences of what became known as the 'Angels of Mons'. The story spread and even became the subject for musical works such as Sydney Baldock's piano solo of the same name. According to the folklorist David Clarke on a far from final analysis, a researcher from the Imperial War Museum concluded: '… to pursue the supporting stories to source is to make a journey into a fog'.

We should, therefore, be very careful with the authenticity of the angel shots shown here. So why have I chosen to include them? The answer is partly, once again, that many, many people believe in such beings; and partly that they raise issues that are worthy of philosophical and moral discussion. If belief in a guardian angel allows a person to avoid taking responsibility for his or her own actions, should we then condone that belief? How do we know that the guardian angel isn't a deceiving demon or a helpful daemon?

If this is becoming somewhat mind-blowing, a return to relative – and it is only relative – normality might be achieved by perusing the image of the red doughnut on page 61: that surely can't be a manifestation of an angel!

The Missing Husband

Receiving recently taken photographs is always a pleasure, since they allow greater scrutiny of the circumstances of the shot and the people concerned. Judith sent this picture along to the publishers with this covering email:

This was a photo of my husband Colin and I on New Year's Eve [2007] with my daughter. There is someone in the background dancing and Colin is overtaken by a bright light that could not have shone through him. He is actually leaning on my right arm.

When I contacted Judith to find out more, she furnished me with plenty of extra details. The shot was taken at a pub in Honiton, Devon, by a friend of Judith's daughter. In this frame her husband was 'blocked out', but in all the other photos he was clearly visible. Judith also told me that her mother had died three days earlier and that they had said their goodbyes during a last visit the week before. Judith believes that her mother's presence may have been with them at the New Year's Eve party and confirmed 'Mum was proud of her two girls (me and my daughter) and loved to have her photo taken with us.' Perhaps her energy has influenced this shot and somehow burnt itself on to the photograph, obliterating Colin from the image in the process.

'her mother had died three days earlier'

The Paranormal Caught on Film

A Hovering Spirit

'Sceptics will advance natural causes such as dust pollution, condensation or lighting anomalies'

This very dark and indistinct photo was taken from a series of infrared digital video shots – five pictures from one second of video – recording a sleep-study session. These images are reminiscent of orbs, but with snake-like activity as opposed to ball movement with trails. There are many photos of orbs available, with varying degrees of clarity and information, and many different opinions about their origins. Sceptics will advance natural causes such as dust pollution, condensation or lighting anomalies, not to mention a deliberate fraud, but I once directed an investigation at the allegedly haunted Bell Hotel in Thetford, Norfolk, where we not only saw orbs with the naked eye but also filmed them in movement. Some religious adherents believe that a soul is revealing itself, others that an astral projection is occurring. Astral projection has been linked with modern studies of out-of-body experiences (OOBEs), notably by the late Arthur Ellison, a professor of electrical engineering, on the positive side and by the psychologist Dr Susan Blackmore from the sceptical viewpoint.

In these images, the effect seems to be moving in a non-random way as if it possessed some kind of will of its own, which may indicate something more than just an odd coincidence of lighting.

A Golden Angel

'he saw a luminous
ball, photographed
it and subsequently
discovered this
angelic form'

An intriguing picture about which we know very little. The only
information I have managed to find is that a Swiss metal-bender called
Silvio took this shot in 1978. Whether he was a metal-bender in the
paranormal sense, like Uri Geller, or a hard-working sheet-metal worker, I
do not know. Evidently Silvio's mother had recently died and whilst taking
a walk in some unspecified woods he saw a luminous ball, photographed
it and subsequently discovered this angelic form. It's another interesting
light effect, but for me, despite the neat 'wings', the angel interpretation
is less credible here. Its form seems rather more random or accidental
than the Michigan Angel on p51 but there is that same quality of
incandescent light again. If it *is* faked, how and why did Silvio indulge in
this subterfuge?

The Ghost of Alton Church

'The long exposure time would certainly produce an effect like this if someone had walked through the shot'

This shot was taken by Eddie Coxton on 12 September 1993 during a flower festival in a church in Staffordshire. Although he admits that there were other people in the church at the time he is adamant that no one was in front of the camera when he took this photograph on a 2–3 second exposure without flash. Questions: did he suffer from photographer's blindness and *did* someone briefly appear in the shot? The long exposure time would certainly produce an effect like this if someone had walked through the shot. Was the print damaged during development? Was the film faulty in the first place? Has the print been doctored to show an apparitional form? Or has Mr Coxton photographed a genuine ghost? Again we come back to the reliability of our information. It is easy to say that there is someone in the exposure. But if you were Mr Coxton and you *knew* there was no one there, what would you think then?

Copyright 1916 by
Dinklier & Blevins

Angel in the Sky

'many people will choose to interpret this cloud formation as a guardian angel'

One Sandy Wasmer provides details of this old photograph on the website www.angelsghosts.com, informing us that:

I have a very old copy of this picture that was found in my grandfather's family bible when he died. Written on the back of the print was "1916 Arthur Hutchens – 4 Wells Kansas"…

Another website (tinet.org) claims it was taken in Oregon by a farmer called Dinklier J Blevins. The latter seems suspicious since the 'J' looks more like an ampersand to me. We are firmly in the realm of the 'Angels of Mons' (see page 37) here and many people will choose to interpret this cloud formation as a guardian angel fighting on the side of the great and the good. As I said in the introduction, if someone receives inspiration or comfort from this belief, there can surely be no objection to it, provided it does no one any harm.

A further explanation for the origin of such images might embrace 'thoughtography', whereby someone is actually imprinting on to the image a thought that is in their minds. This theory may sound bizarre, but is it any odder than the idea that there are angels fluttering around our skies?

The Legend of Highgate Cemetery

'There have often been stories of vampires associated with the area'

Highgate Cemetery in North London has a great deal of history and superstition attached to it. It was built in 1839 to relieve the overcrowded churchyards within the city and now covers 14 hectares (37 acres) of Grade Two listed parkland. There are 51,000 graves, with 850 classed as notable, including those of Karl Marx and Michael Faraday.

There have often been stories of vampires associated with the area. This photo was taken in November 1994 and nothing unusual was noticed at the time. However, on development, a strange, nebulous figure was noticed in the foreground. The negative was then sent to Maurice Grosse at the SPR, who was baffled. Is it possible that the effect was caused by chemical staining or even a defect in the original film or is it the appearance of something paranormal? It has not been possible to find the photographer – so if you know who it was, please get in touch!

Shimmering Angel

This image was sent to the website ghoststudy.com. It was evidently taken with a digital camera in Rockford, Michigan, and the person over whom the angel appears to be hovering was due to have surgery the next day. We are told that 'prayers were being said for a fast recovery' as the picture was taken.

The power of prayer has been commented on in many religious works and, indeed, I published an article myself comparing its veridical potential with that of spells undertaken by contemporary witches and Wiccans. Many people believe in the existence of guardian angels, be they discarnate (that is, disembodied) entities, religious manifestations or parts of their own psyche.

I discussed this image with a photographer and we agreed that there were two reasons to be suspicious about it: firstly, as with so many modern images, it could easily have been tampered with and the tampering, if done by an expert, would not be readily detectable; and secondly, the suggestion of a guardian angel shows a lack of objectivity. The photographer wondered why Scott, when submitting the photograph to the website, had not invited suggestions rather than dictating the image's angelic provenance. However, there is no denying the angelic form that the image takes, and the quality of the light is so strikingly similar to 'The Missing Husband' image on page 39 that perhaps there really was an angel watching over these people that day.

'the person over whom the angel appears to be hovering was due to have surgery the next day'

Bachelor's Grove Mist

Readers of *Ghosts Caught on Film* will be aware of some of the history
and hauntings attached to this cemetery in Illinois, and over the years
mysterious mists have also been filmed which people have claimed have
not been attributable to weather conditions or breath being photographed
accidentally. There have been a number of investigations, with different
types of anomaly reported. Such mists are quite common either in
conjunction with other paranormal events, as in the case of Belgrave
Hall, Leicester (also discussed in *Ghosts Caught on Film*), or as a separate
manifestation. These have included poltergeist activity (objects moving of
their own accord) and alleged apparitions. A few years ago I attended a vigil
at a derelict but allegedly haunted church in Essex and was able to video one
such mist. I attributed this to the weather being conducive to such conditions,
but a colleague believed it to be paranormal. Who is to say he was wrong
and I was right or vice versa?

'mysterious mists
have also been
filmed which people
have claimed
have not been
attributable to
weather conditions'

The Cypriot Ghost

'he is adamant that
nobody crossed in
front of the wall
where his camera
was positioned'

George Kanigowski took this shot of the harbour lights at
Limassol Bay on the night of 23 September 1986, when
the temperature was about 29°C (84°F). He is able to be
very particular about the circumstances of the shot (being
taken on an Olympus OM10 camera on a tripod with 25
ASA Kodachrome film on a 30-second exposure without
flash). He says he took five shots, each about two minutes
apart, and he is adamant that nobody crossed in front of
the wall where his camera was positioned. His girlfriend
was with him at the time and verifies this. Although most
of George's shots appeared normal after processing by
Kodak back in England, one seems to contain an unknown
effect. The lighting anomaly has a similar quality to the
angel captured in St Peter's Basilica (see page 63) but that
was apparently created by strong daylight – the source of
this apparition is not so obvious.

A History of Pain

'one of the orphans
whose ghost is said
to roam the cloisters'

This intriguing image was taken by members of the Haunted Britain investigation team at the Royal Victoria Patriotic Building in South London. The eerie swirls of light look as if they may simply have been caused by the camera moving during the taking of the picture, but not only do the team claim that this was not the case, but the camera was actually mounted on a tripod at the time, and therefore incapable of movement.

The building itself has an intriguing past: built as an orphanage for daughters of servicemen who died in the Crimean War, it was nearly closed down following a scandal involving the abuse and death of one of the orphans whose ghost is said to roam the cloisters. During the First World War it was used as a military hospital; the field behind the building, now the cricket pitch, was filled with marquees housing as many as 1800 patients at any one time. During the Second World War the building became an alien clearing station run by MI6. It was rumoured that suspected spies were incarcerated for years, both in the building and in windowless concrete cells constructed in the south courtyard. So there's plenty of background for paranormal activity, but perhaps not enough to go on with these strange lights to speculate further.

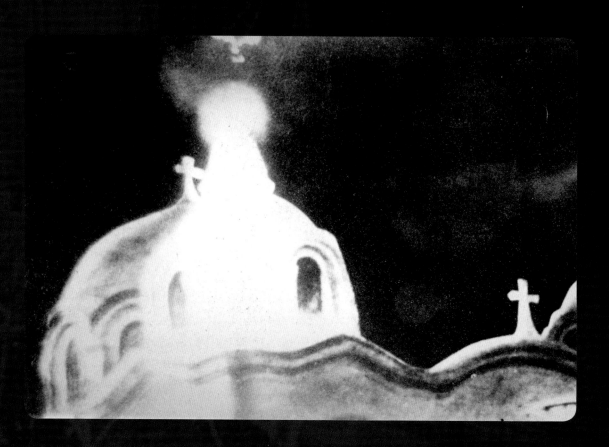

The Virgin in Egypt

'If this was a carefully planned hoax one hopes that it would have been discovered and the perpetrators unmasked'

Visions of the Virgin Mary are numerous – Lourdes in France and Knock in Eire spring to mind – and she seems to appear in a number of guises, ranging from firm simulacra such as rocks and trees to water-based or aerial projections. We have photographic evidence for one of the more famous examples of the latter taken in 1968, showing what looks like a version of the Virgin Mary over the Coptic orthodox church of St Mary in Zeitoun, Egypt. The Virgin allegedly stayed there for some ten days and was seen by hundreds of people. If this was a carefully planned hoax one hopes that it would have been discovered and the perpetrators unmasked, but no such dénouement took place.

Mary appeared again in Cairo in 1986, coinciding with extensive power failures (not uncommon in Cairo at any time) and political upheavals. A sign from God; an elaborate hoax; a natural light/ cloud formation? Again, it's for you to decide.

The Mysterious Red Doughnut

This is another of the many photographs of bizarre images that were sent to Maurice Grosse between 1977 and 2006. It was taken as a family shot of two children under perfectly normal circumstances in their garden in Stafford in 1994. Other photographs on the same film did not contain any unusual markings. However, the large red shape is quite unmistakable and almost seems to fit beneath the girl's arm. It has been suggested to me that the photographer's first finger and thumb might accidentally have been caught in the shot, but since cameras usually have the shutter button on the right hand side this would have made holding the camera very difficult. Furthermore, the colour would not seem to be appropriate. The 'camera strap' syndrome is often blamed for unaccountable shapes on the edge of photographs, but I don't think that works in this case. One commentator, perhaps with a degree of humour, suggested the image resembled a 'scrunchy' (a piece of elasticated material that holds long hair in place) that might have flown partially in front of the lens. With this example it has not been possible to view the negative to see if the red image is different there or to check for tampering.

'Other photographs on the same film did not contain any unusual markings'

Angel in the Vatican

'The blurred figure may suggest an angel'

This photo caused quite a storm when it appeared in the *Daily Express* on 31 March 2007. It was taken by Andy Key, a retired policeman, when he was visiting the Vatican and listening to the Pope in St Peter's Basilica. Neither he nor anyone else observed the figure and it was only when he and his wife viewed the shots on his computer after returning home that they noticed the anomaly. The blurred figure may suggest an angel, but only in its traditional appearance of a winged being, impregnated on our minds through Renaissance artworks. Mr Key alleges that professional photographers were baffled as to what caused it, but it seems likely to be a coincidental play of light and reflections from the window above. Mr Key also stressed that he and his wife were not in Rome for religious reasons but simply sightseeing. But the resemblance of the apparition to an angel greatly adds to its power in a place of such religious significance.

SIMULACRA

My edition of *The Penguin English Dictionary* succinctly defines 'simulacrum' as a 'deceptive representation', but one needs to expand this here since the possibilities for finding simulacra are endless. One explanation suggests the concept of pareidolia, which the sceptic Robert Todd Carroll describes as:

A type of illusion or misperception involving a vague or obscure stimulus being perceived as something clear and distinct. For example, in the discolourations of a burnt tortilla one sees the face of Jesus Christ. Or one sees the image of Mother Teresa in a cinnamon bun, or the Virgin Mary in the bark of a tree.

From a vast store of possibilities I have included in this chapter examples of cloud formation, trees, rocks, wood, flower petals, glass reflections, concrete and even a baby scan. Religious imagery appears frequently, with the Virgin Mary and Jesus topping the bill, so to speak. As our brains try to make sense of our surroundings it is to be expected that we seek to translate everything we perceive into known images. There are anecdotal accounts of explorers' ships being invisible to the inhabitants of undiscovered shores as they approached, because the concept of a vast galleon was beyond the scope of the people's imaginations. There are many books devoted to the subject of optical illusions and we are all aware of the mirages caused by extreme weather conditions in the desert. A visit to an Imax 3D cinema will soon confirm our conditioning as we duck to avoid pterodactyls or spears thrown by enemy 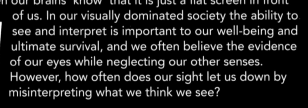 armies when our brains 'know' that it is just a flat screen in front of us. In our visually dominated society the ability to see and interpret is important to our well-being and ultimate survival, and we often believe the evidence of our eyes while neglecting our other senses. However, how often does our sight let us down by misinterpreting what we think we see?

So why devote a chapter to phenomena that are probably *not* paranormal? The simple answer is that many people believe that simulacra appear in order to convey a message either to an individual or to mankind as a whole. In a secular society it is easy to dismiss

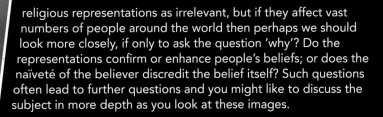

religious representations as irrelevant, but if they affect vast numbers of people around the world then perhaps we should look more closely, if only to ask the question 'why'? Do the representations confirm or enhance people's beliefs; or does the naïveté of the believer discredit the belief itself? Such questions often lead to further questions and you might like to discuss the subject in more depth as you look at these images.

Of course, not all the photographs concern religious icons; a further Pandora's box could be opened about the famous 'face on Mars' image and the lesser-known statue-like figure – both shown in this chapter. I have a rather mischievous picture in my mind of space scientists tearing their hair out as the good and the great queue up to tell them these figures are not simply rock semblances of humans, but signs of life on Mars or evidence of earlier civilizations. The debate must point out that scientists have made some spectacular mistakes in the past and it would be so much more interesting if they were wrong on this occasion too!

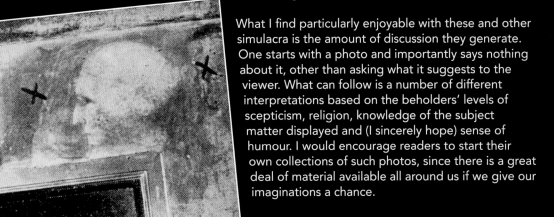

What I find particularly enjoyable with these and other simulacra is the amount of discussion they generate. One starts with a photo and importantly says nothing about it, other than asking what it suggests to the viewer. What can follow is a number of different interpretations based on the beholders' levels of scepticism, religion, knowledge of the subject matter displayed and (I sincerely hope) sense of humour. I would encourage readers to start their own collections of such photos, since there is a great deal of material available all around us if we give our imaginations a chance.

Baby Scan or Baby Scam?

Ultrasound images of unborn babies like this will be familiar to parents everywhere, but this one comes with something extra. The scan is of Laurna Turner's unborn child, taken in Birmingham, England, in 2006 and appears to show the face of Jesus in the left centre. Finding such an image in a tree trunk or a stain on the wall is one thing, but imagine your feelings if the ultrasound scan of your baby appeared to show the image of Christ!

An eerie aside to this picture is that I found it in the archives of the agency Rex Features, the copy I saw bearing the word 'Rex' just above the image of Jesus ('rex' being the Latin word for 'king' and often applied to Jesus, for instance as in 'King of the Jews'). A simple coincidence but it gave me quite a shock nevertheless.

As far as I know, the story ends there. We can only assume that there was nothing unusual about the conception of Laurna's baby and I don't recall astronomers getting excited about any unusual activity in the night sky over Birmingham later that year.

'imagine your feelings if the ultrasound scan of your baby appeared to show the image of Christ!'

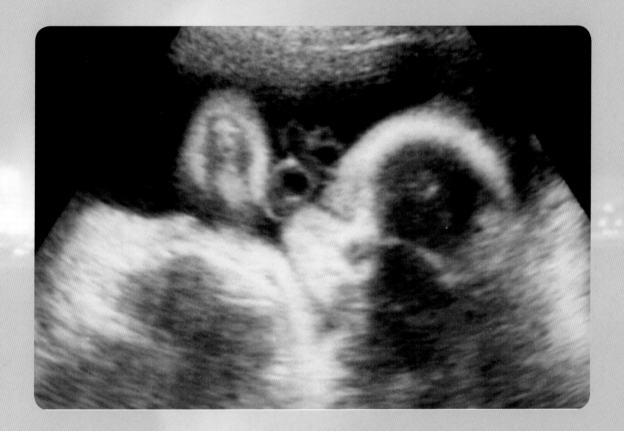

The Plate-Glass Virgin

'this did not stop many people visiting the building and setting up shrines and vigils'

The ever-popular Virgin Mary appeared yet again, this time in the glass of the Seminole Finance building in Clearwater, Florida, in November and December 1996. Although agnostics provided what they thought to be logical explanations for the image – namely water reflections or chemical deposits – this did not stop many people visiting the building and setting up shrines and vigils, believing that this was a sign from heaven. The incident subsequently received further publicity when nuns from the St Anne Order in Bangalore, India, confirmed its importance. When the weather and temperature changed, the vision disappeared from sight, presumably to reappear equally miraculously in another location. However you choose to interpret it, the image was thought-provoking enough for people to consider its message and decide on its authenticity accordingly.

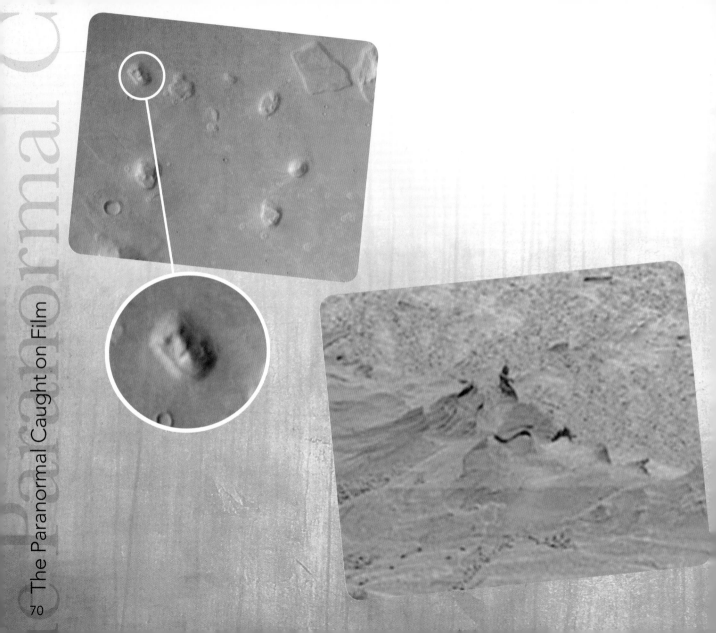

Mars Mysteries

These controversial images are from the planet Mars. The first one was taken by the NASA spacecraft *Viking I* in 1976, in the region of Mars known as Cydonia and appears to show a face or mask; the other, taken by the Mars rover *Spirit* in 2004, appears to show a statue or a crouching figure.

With these images one is forced to choose between two conflicting interpretations. Richard Hoagland's *The Mars Mission* would have you believe that these structures were laid out by an alien civilization, that they convey a message to the inhabitants of Earth and that various sacred sites such as the Egyptian Sphinx and Avebury stone circle are connected to them in geometrical ways. A belief in conspiracy theories allows one to take the view that NASA may even agree with these revelations, but for political reasons is not allowed to disturb the world with its findings. A perhaps satirical (or worryingly perhaps not!) interpretation is offered by those claiming the second image to be a garden gnome, the Virgin Mary, Bigfoot or even a precursor of the Little Mermaid statue in Copenhagen. The opposing view, held by so-called 'hard' scientists, is that the formations are not manmade but are tricks of light and shadow; that they do not convey any sort of message and that they have been misinterpreted in line with the standard pareidolia principles of trying to find recognizable patterns in randomized configurations. The 'Man in the Moon' is a well-known example. You, the viewer, may wish to devise other possibilities.

'they convey a message to the inhabitants of Earth'

Madonna & Child Over the Rainbow

'An unknown friend
later pointed out the
anomaly in the sky'

Not possessing either original photographs or negatives is the bane of serious researchers of alleged photographic anomalies. This is one such example and is accordingly reliant upon indirect testimonies. One Ivy Wilson is said to have taken this shot of a rainbow at her home near Woombye, Queensland, Australia, in 1980. An unknown friend later pointed out the anomaly in the sky, suggesting that it could have been a reflection on glass from a statue in the house. Mrs Wilson maintained that the photograph was taken outside and that she owned no such statues.

By way of a sequel to this event, the seer Susanna d'Amore later maintained that she had been led to the place by the spirit of the stigmatic Padre Pio (see the chapter, 'The Unexplained: Poltergeists & Other Phenomena', page 92, for more on stigmatism): 'She claimed a close encounter with the Blessed Virgin Mary there, bought a few acres of land at the site, and built a small chapel. She discovered a small spring whose water was believed to have healing qualities, and busloads of pilgrims began to arrive, some of whom claimed to witness "the miracle of the sun".'

Tree Spirit

This bizarre photo was sent to the psychical investigator and professional photographer Cyril Permutt in the late 1970s and it is housed in the SPR Archive, together with many other intriguing photographs. There are different ways of interpreting the image according to one's belief system. As we have seen before, the sceptic will claim it is simply a double exposure or simulacrum, of which there are many examples to be found in gnarled tree trunks. However, some pagan religions allocate entities to all aspects of nature, specifically earth, air, fire and water. Furthermore, pantheistic beliefs credit trees with having their own 'souls' (for want of a better word), which may become visible at unknown times and in unknown circumstances. A believer in pagan elementals could therefore easily be persuaded that a tree spirit had been caught on film here. Just because such appearances are extremely rare, should we discount them all as unacceptable?

'pantheistic beliefs credit trees with having their own "souls" '

The Virgin of the Rose Petals

Yet another instance of the Virgin Mary and Jesus appearing in unusual guises, this time in 1948, when rose petals bearing their images evidently dropped from the sky at a Carmelite convent in Lipa City in the Philippines. A novice called Teresita Castillo was allegedly contacted by an apparition of the Virgin and various paranormal phenomena occurred. The formal church took exception to this and the convent was 'sealed'. However, in 1990 there was a new outbreak of religious fervour – a white luminous outline of a female in prayer began to appear on one of the leaves of a tall coconut tree. A year later, rose petals began to fall straight from the sky again and six children playing in the garden at the convent saw a statue come to life. If you find yourself in the Philippines you might like to check this out. The address is Shrine of Our Lady Mary, Mediatrix of All Grace, Torres St, Antipola, Lipa City, Batangas. Good luck!

'Teresita Castillo was allegedly contacted by an apparition of the Virgin and various paranormal phenomena occurred'

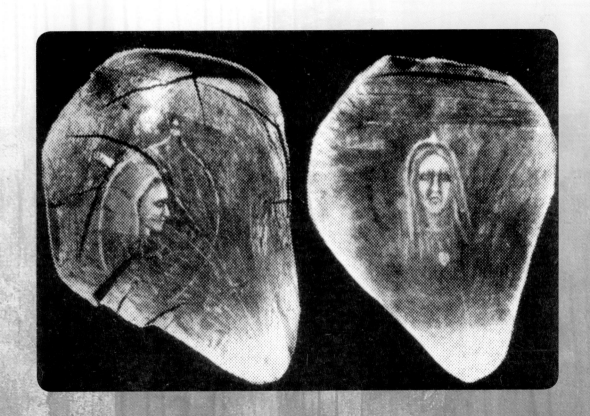

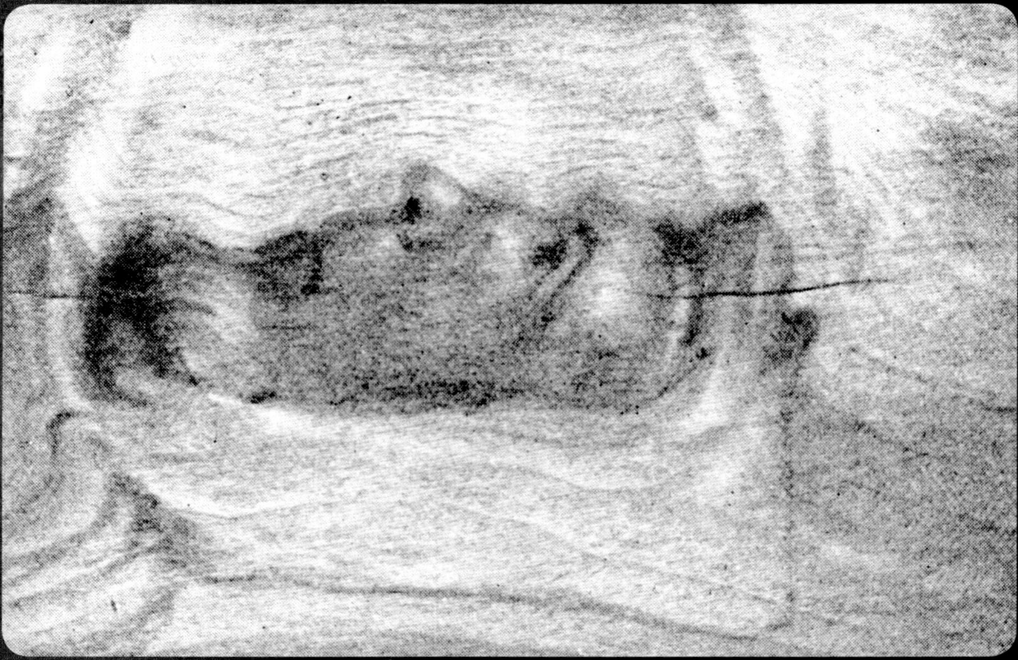

The Poplar Face

'one can ... indulge in some imaginative scenario involving a spirit of the woods'

This image was found in a plank of poplar wood from the mountains of West Virginia, USA, in October 1894. It is such an exceptionally clear representation of a hooded, bearded man that one wonders whether it has been doctored in some way either directly onto the wood or via the photo itself. Given the technical limitations of nineteenth-century photography, I think the latter unlikely, although the general public's ignorance of the photographic medium in its earlier days did lead to some fairly blatant, and what we would consider crude, hoaxes such as the Cottingley Fairies (see *Ghosts Caught on Film*). If, however, the face is genuine, then one can either accept it as a pleasant coincidence or indulge in some imaginative scenario involving a spirit of the woods leaving an imprint for all to see. It might, for instance, be argued that a local woodsman who either worked or died in the area manifested himself in this way as a reminder of his existence. But perhaps this stretches credulity too much.

The Face in the Cathedral

Images have appeared in stone for many years and when they have either resembled people associated with the place or have been so lifelike as to be undeniable faces – as for instance was the case at Belmez (see *Ghosts Caught on Film*) – they have been worthy of investigation. *Fortean Times* often prints such pictures, which have included such notables as Jesus Christ and Lady Diana – the latter in concrete, no less! The image here, from the same source, is from Christ Church Cathedral, Oxford, England, and purports to show Dean Liddell, the father of Lewis Carroll's Alice, who died in 1898. Furthermore, it is claimed that other faces also appeared near to that of the Dean. Damp walls often provide 'recognizable' images that the brain can process easily and once one has noticed a resemblance it is difficult to rid oneself of that interpretation. More positively, one might accept that these phenomena are genuine signs from unknown sources that appear now and then to extend our thought processes and beliefs.

'The image here ... purports to show Dean Liddell, the father of Lewis Carroll's Alice'

The Madonna of the Rocks

'It bears an extraordinary resemblance to traditional figures of the Madonna carrying the Christ-child'

This rocky crag near Naples in Italy was photographed by Nick Yates of Brighouse in Yorkshire, England. It bears an extraordinary resemblance to traditional figures of the Madonna carrying the Christ-child, with Christ in this case apparently wearing a prominent crown, the 'crown' being the branches of a tree sprouting from the cliff. In fact it has been suggested that it actually looks more like the Virgin carrying a small stag than the baby Jesus, but this minor defect in an otherwise fascinating simulacrum is doubtless not enough to deter the faithful from seeing the divine in this work of nature.

Giant Ice Ghost

With simulacra we always need to maintain a balance between those that provoke serious thoughts and those that, however startling they may be, are open to a humorous interpretation. This picture is an obvious example of the latter; it was taken in Hocking Hills, Ohio, USA, and subsequently sent to the website ghoststudy.com. The comparative size of the figure in front of this ice formation indicates that the 'ghost' is quite a giant. It also looks just the way a fun ghost should look – one can almost hear it go 'boo'!

'It also looks just the way a fun ghost should look'

The Virgin in the Subway

'even in what many believe to be a secular society, religious beliefs and superstitions lurk just below the surface'

The date is 19 April 2005; the place is the Kennedy Expressway underpass, Chicago, Illinois, USA; the miracle is that a yellow and white stain on the concrete wall has formed itself into an image of the Virgin Mary on the day that Cardinal Joseph Ratzinger is elected Pope Benedict XVI. In reality the image was discovered the day before and then hysteria or curiosity took over, leading hundreds of people to visit the spot to leave flowers, candles and prayers. It is remarkable how demonstrative people become in response to this sort of occurrence. Perhaps it indicates that, even in what many believe to be a secular society, religious beliefs and superstitions lurk just below the surface.

Stains in concrete have appeared at various times as so-called paranormal phenomena: perhaps in some ways they have replaced the older 'significant' blood stains that couldn't be removed when a grisly crime had been committed. It is not my business to comment on people's belief systems; if they are happy to believe that Mary is contacting the world via a Chicago underpass then, if it does no harm to them or to others, so be it.

The Sleeping Woman

Some of the commonest and often most compelling simulacra are provided by the contours of trees and rocks. A good example is this 'sleeping woman' from Studley Royal Park in North Yorkshire, England, photographed by John Billingsley. Paranormal? Probably not, but one could argue that the tree produced this shape for a specific reason and that it was not a random growth, especially if the apparent image was meaningful to the viewer.

'one could argue that the tree produced this shape for a specific reason'

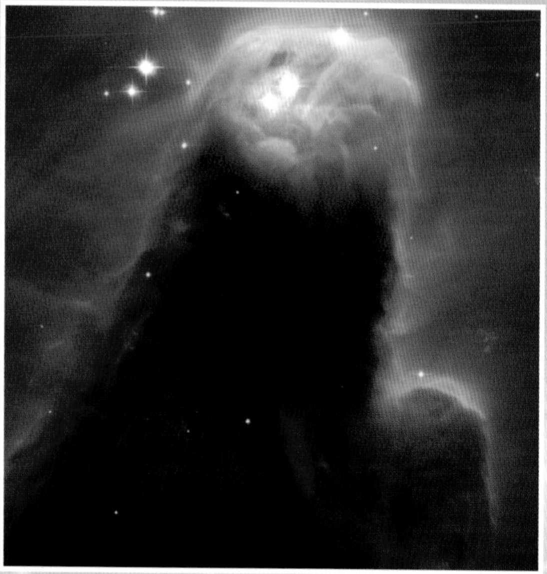

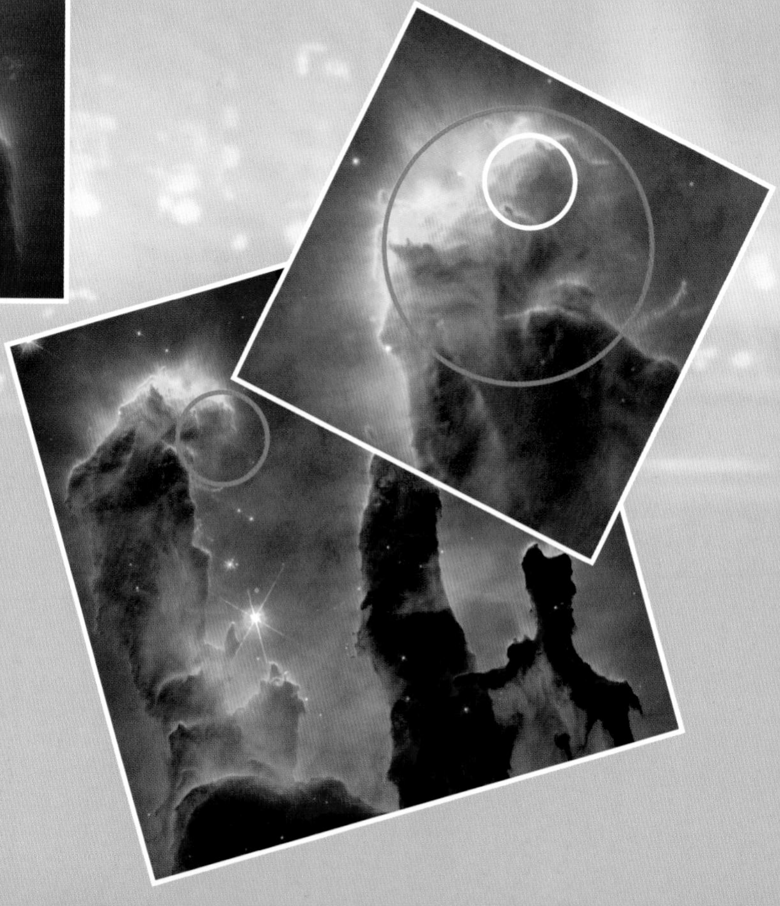

Images in the Heavens

The Hubble Space Telescope has revolutionized our view of the universe since it first started collecting data from the depths of the cosmos in 1990. It was perhaps inevitable that some people would look for and find divine meaning in these images and, sure enough, here are two examples of 'the face of Jesus' in deep space.

The first is the Cone Nebula – the lighter areas of gas cloud defining a mane of hair and shoulder, but the face, or where the face should be, is featureless darkness. In the Eagle Nebula the 'face' is more interesting. The towering pillars are formed from molecular hydrogen gas and dust and, rather fittingly, provide the conditions for the birth of new stars. At the peak of one of these pillars, once the image has been rotated 90 degrees, a recognizable face does appear on close inspection. What gets believers excited is this verse from the Gospel according to Matthew:

And then shall appear the sign of the Son of man in heaven: and then shall all the tribes of the earth mourn, and they shall see the Son of man coming in the clouds of heaven with power and great glory.

I am always one to advocate keeping an open mind, but on the other hand we should be careful not to remain so open-minded that our brains fall out!

'The towering pillars ... rather fittingly provide the conditions for the birth of new stars'

THE UNEXPLAINED: POLTERGEISTS & OTHER PHENOMENA

This is not quite a miscellaneous chapter, since a number of extremely interesting phenomena have been omitted. I hope that a future book may explore two very different worlds, namely those of the UFO and of cryptozoology, neither of which appears here. Instead we maintain a distinctly human emphasis, albeit in strange situations. The first is the phenomenon of the poltergeist, or noisy spirit. I have a particular interest here since I have witnessed poltergeist activity first hand and also had the privilege of undertaking a detailed study of the original documents and hundreds of hours of audio tape connected with the Enfield poltergeist (see page 95).

A return to occurrences connected with Christianity can be found in the examples of stigmata and alleged bleeding statues. The phenomenon of people displaying Christ's wounds is not new, but what makes it more interesting in the present day is the knowledge that forensic medical science can bring to the subject, as well as surveillance techniques to expose self-infliction. It seems possible, even likely, that in the relatively near future stigmatism will be understood as a psychosomatic condition, albeit a rare one, that can be treated, if desired, with surgery or drugs. Of course, some stigmatists consider themselves to be blessed rather than suffering, so they may well refuse medical help. The many hundreds of bleeding, oozing, weeping etc. statues from around the world can be investigated when permission is given. This can allow us to discover whether the emanations are unknown substances or melting paint, varnish, mineral deposits and the like occurring naturally or being introduced fraudulently to evoke greater belief in worshippers – and perhaps solicit donations.

The human body is a complicated organism and although we know far more about it now than we did even a few years ago, it would be ludicrous to suggest that our knowledge is complete. The mysterious auras that can be captured with specialist photography, with varying interpretations attached to the different colours, come into this category, as does the ominous predicament of spontaneous human combustion. There are several well-documented cases of the latter, and plenty of disagreement amongst experts as to whether it can happen and if so how. It would be interesting to ask a fireman for his views on whether a body can be reduced to ashes by a normal coal or wood fire, yet leave flammable objects and materials undamaged close by.

The final category in this chapter concerns our desire to fly or to defy gravity without pre-prepared environments or special equipment. Our society provides us with flying 'superheroes' like Superman and Batman; we also sometimes fly in our dreams and, if we believe the countless witnesses recorded in both folklore and history, some people do it by entering an altered state of consciousness. Flying has been a mixed blessing in the numerous examples recorded in church history, since angels and demons, saints and witches can all fly but have evoked somewhat different responses from the religions concerned. It would appear that some Buddhists and yogic practitioners can bounce higher than they should naturally be able to, and Spiritualism had its famous authenticated levitator in the person of Daniel Dunglas Home in nineteenth-century London. The Indian rope trick has been largely discredited and stage magicians have shown that they can reproduce virtually everything that can be achieved with alleged paranormal powers, but the fact that something can be replicated by conjuring skills does not mean that deception is employed every time it is done. Perhaps the people who genuinely possess these skills keep well away from the public eye to avoid the media attention and the constant testing in unnatural circumstances to which they would be submitted. If so, who can blame them?

The Enfield Poltergeist

The Enfield Poltergeist case was possibly the most thoroughly investigated paranormal event of the latter half of the twentieth century. The activities at a small house in Enfield, Middlesex, England, were extremely well documented over a period of more than a year around 1977 and have caused a great deal of controversy since. In this short space I can only give a tiny flavour of what happened: a serious researcher should read Playfair's *This House is Haunted* (1980) or examine the Maurice Grosse file which is part of the Society for Psychical Research Archives held at Cambridge University Library.

Briefly, inexplicable noises alerted the family to poltergeist activity that seemed to be particularly focused on one of the daughters, Janet, aged 11, and to a lesser extent her sister Margaret, who was 13. Neighbours, the police, journalists and finally psychical investigators were brought in to try to authenticate the events. This culminated in a large number of well-witnessed manifestations, including the movement of large pieces of furniture and other objects; Janet's levitation; the outbreak of inexplicable fires; and most spectacularly of all a gruff male voice – similar in some ways to Regan's voice in the film *The Exorcist* – coming from both girls.

To this day, on the rare occasions that Janet and Margaret are willing to talk about the events of 30 years ago, they maintain that the phenomena were genuine. I have personally spent a great deal of time both in conversation with the investigators and correlating the Enfield files for the SPR archive and I believe that at least some of the manifestations were real. Whether these photos of Janet levitating were part of that reality is for the viewer to decide.

'This culminated in a large number of well-witnessed manifestations'

Spontaneous Human Combustion

There has been much discussion and controversy concerning the existence of spontaneous human combustion (SHC) since Dickens mentioned it in *Bleak House*. A standard definition of this usually fatal condition is that the body seems to be consumed by fire without the involvement of an external agent. Often a part of the body, clothing or surrounding material is not burned. In some cases survivors have spoken of a fire seeming to come from within them and this has even been corroborated after medical examination. Experts in the nature and effects of fire have often disagreed and it is possible that some mysterious deaths by fire might be examples of SHC. Sceptics usually maintain that outside natural causes are to blame, which is strongly in opposition to the belief in psychosomatic suicide or some kind of demonic integration, whereby unknown occult practices cause the body to conflagrate in extreme circumstances currently beyond our understanding.

Numerous articles in publications such as the *Journal of the Society for Psychical Research*, *Fate Magazine* and *Fortean Times*, as well as the occasional television documentary, draw attention to SHC. Reported cases come from numerous countries and involve people from a variety of backgrounds. One well-known example was that of Dr John Thomas Bentley, who died in Pennsylvania, USA, in 1966. All that remained of him was a part of one lower leg with a foot and shoe intact.

The disturbing image reproduced here shows the aftermath of the death by fire of Ms E M, who was found in this state in London on 29 January 1958. She appears to have fallen into the fire, but the heat generated in an ordinary fire such as this would not be sufficient to reduce a body to ash. Other items close by, including a wooden chair and some textiles, do not seem to be affected. For a first-hand description of this phenomenon by John Heymer the interested reader should see *New Scientist*, 15 May 1986.

'when the victims have survived they have spoken of the fire seeming to come from within them'

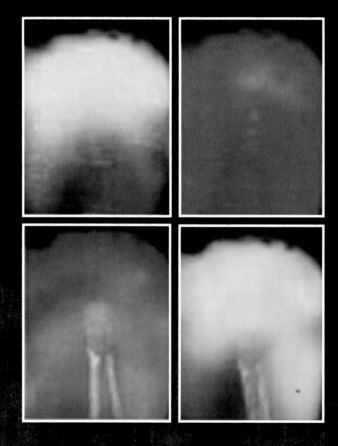

A Colourful Aura

The photographing of auras and the interpretation of the different colours still causes controversy and disagreement. My personal preference for purple was not manifested when I was photographed using this technique, since I was surrounded and to a large extent obliterated by the colour red. I was told it meant I had psychic abilities that I was blocking because of my 'sceptical nature'. The example presented here from Danièle Laurent provides quite a contrast to that shot of me, since a distinct image of the head and shoulders can be seen surrounded by purple and blue light. Different interpreters – or in some cases mediums – accord different meanings to different colours, which can indicate a range of aspects of the sitter's health and personality.

The photos were taken using a Polaroid camera while the subjects' fingers were resting on the electric 'plate' that allowed their auras to be manifested and captured on film. (Having been photographed this way myself, I can vouch for the fact that no pain is felt.) To obtain an auric photograph of yourself you might attend a Mind, Body, Spirit conference, where such things are often available.

'a distinct image of the head and shoulders can be seen surrounded by purple and blue light'

Yogic Flying

This is a practitioner of so-called 'yogic flying', a form of near-levitation carried out by followers of the Maharishi Mahesh Yogi and his form of Transcendental Meditation. There are various ways of interpreting what is happening here. A practitioner of yoga would argue that, as the mind and the body combine in an altered state of consciousness, the resulting lightness of spirit and body allows the body to bounce higher in the air than it would normally be able to do. Physical synchronicity is all-important both here and in the common party trick of lifting someone into the air using four people's fingertips, something I have done on many occasions. However, an opposing viewpoint might argue that the athleticism and flexibility of a fit and healthy human body could achieve this effect without the need for the yogic dimension. This photograph certainly makes the method look quite successful but the only moving film I have seen of the practice looks a lot more like hopping than flying. According to one practitioner it works like this:

People would rock gently, then more and more, and then start lifting off into the air. You should really be in a lotus position to do it – you can hurt yourself landing if you've got a dangling undercarriage. To begin with it's like the Wright brothers' first flight – you come down with a bump. That's why we have to sit on foam rubber cushions. Then you learn to control it better, and it becomes totally exhilarating.
(*Unexplained*, Volume 2, page 347, 1981)

'the resulting lightness of spirit and body allows the body to bounce higher in the air'

The Diabolical Poltergeist

This photograph purports to show some of the poltergeist damage that took place in the suburbs of Sao Paulo, Brazil, over an 11-year period from 1973–84. The slashing of the furniture is visible here, but other reported phenomena included spontaneous fires, the appearance of apports (objects that should not have normally been present, such as rosemary branches and crossed swords), objects being hurled around, possession trances, apparitions, physical attacks on the family involved and 'monster-like appearances' in which the 'monsters' were said to have the characteristics of werewolves. The events were reported in 1984 with mentions of 'discarnate agents' (phenomena that are not recognized by current science or nature) and 'black magic rites'. Various exorcisms were conducted and other checks were performed but failed to discover any evidence of fraud. The whole case was written up in detail by Michel-Ange Amorim in the *Journal of the Society for Psychical Research*, volume 56, 1990. Significantly the author preferred a 'living agent' hypothesis to one of the paranormal, but further correspondence followed on after the case had been terminated. The main investigator's view was challenged by other researchers who also had experience in these types of phenomena. People in the vicinity witnessed the occurrences first hand and they were in little doubt about their 'diabolical' origin.

'objects being hurled around, possession trances, apparitions, physical attacks ... and "monster-like appearances" '

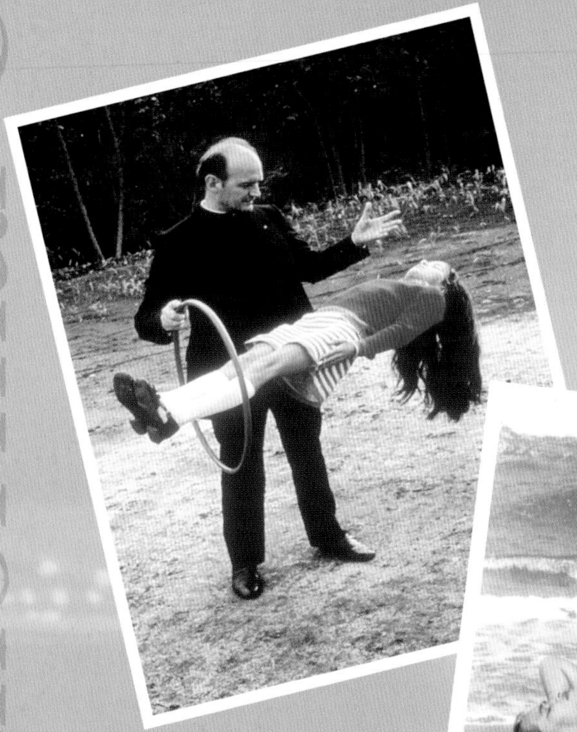

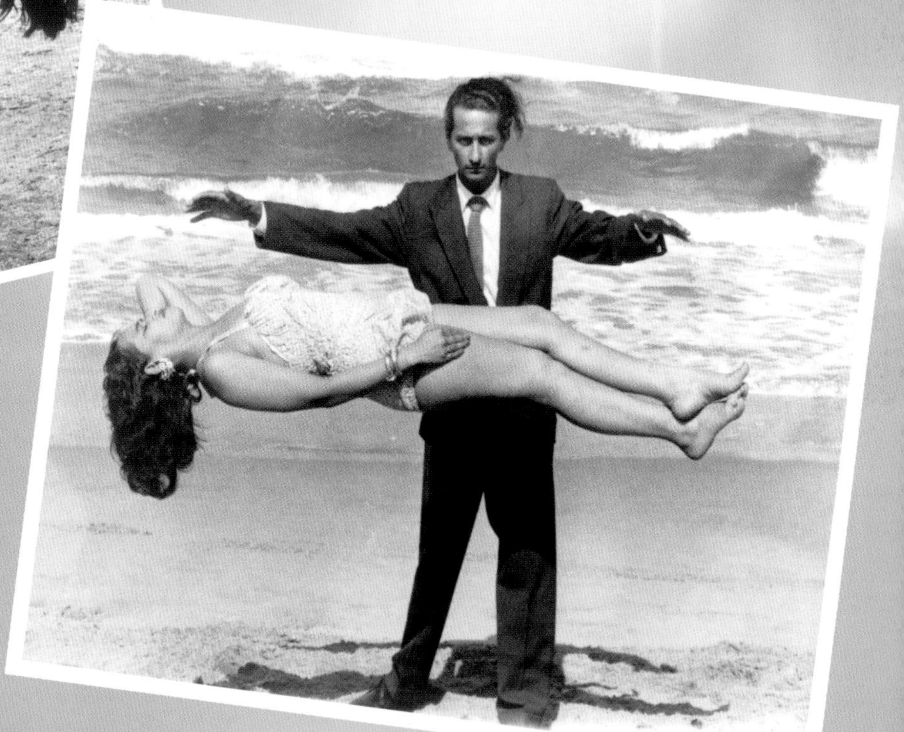

The Levitators

There are many examples of levitation from historical and folkloric sources and if just one of them is correct then we are left with a phenomenon that is not meant to exist … but does! The list of possible levitators includes such famous mediums as Daniel Dunglas Home and a bevy of saints including Joseph of Copertino and Teresa of Avila. A stage magician – David Copperfield comes to mind here – might maintain that levitation is a trick and that with the correct devices and knowledge anyone can do it, whatever their state of mind. Perhaps psychology would emphasize the illusory nature of the phenomenon, suggesting that the body isn't really levitating but that the minds of both levitator and observer believe it is.

The two pictures shown here provide, at the very least, food for thought. In the first we see the Jesuit and investigator of the paranormal Father Quevedo performing levitation with a child: it may well be that he is demonstrating how easy it is to fool a gullible viewer. The other picture shows the Indian stage magician Yusultini and his wife Faeeza performing a levitation trick on a beach near Durban in South Africa. This photo has not been faked and there are none of the supporting wires or cables regularly assumed to be used in stage magic. Yusultini assures us that it is a trick, but he won't say how he does it!

'Yusultini assures us that it is a trick, but he won't say how he does it!'

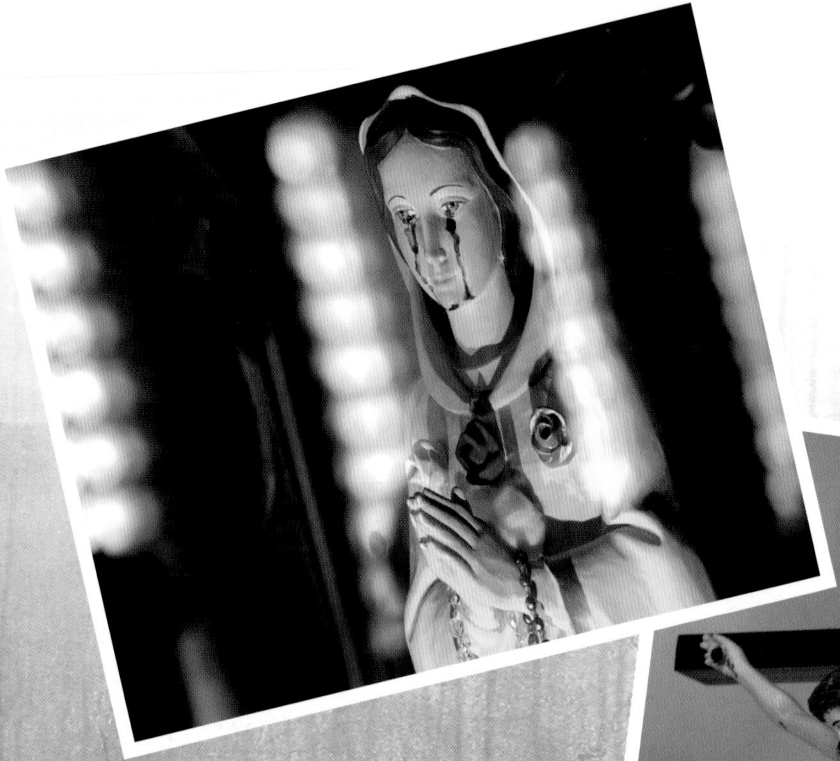

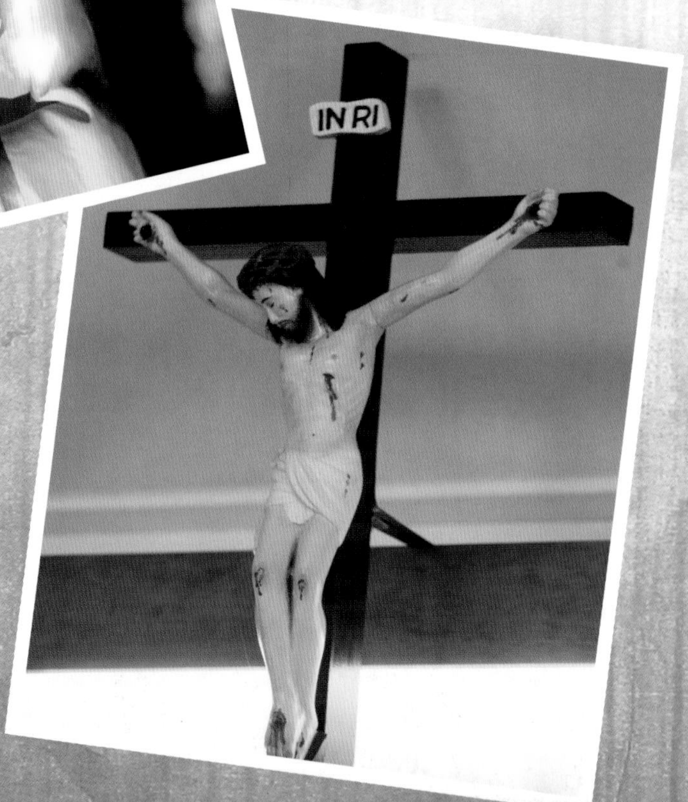
INRI

Divine Blood & Tears

There is a huge choice available for readers who are interested in pursuing the phenomenon of weeping or bleeding statues of the Virgin Mary. *Fortean Times* is a good source of information on a range of examples, including the 'Weeping Virgin of Civitavecchia', the 'Weeping Virgin of Guadeloupe' and the 'Bleeding Madonna of Grangecon, County Wicklow'. The example chosen here, photographed on 20 March 2003, is generally known as the 'Weeping Virgin of Caracas, Venezuela'. Through an unpleasant coincidence the statue in San Cayetano Church started oozing in December 2002, a few days after a rally there where gunmen had killed three people, one of whom had been baptized in the church. The local priest, Father José Coromoto, reported that an invalid woman could walk freely after praying to the statue.

The crucifix pictured was photographed in the Vietnamese Catholic Church in Inala, Brisbane, Australia, on 27 May 2004 and allegedly shows Jesus weeping oil.

So what causes these exudations? One explanation, put forward by chemists, is that a hollow statue made out of porous matter can be filled with liquid, which will be sealed in after the outer shell has been glazed. If the glaze is then scratched, near the eyes for instance, the liquid will dribble out, resembling tear drops. Other possibilities are discoloured drips, perhaps from a ceiling, falling onto a statue or alterations in the statue's chemical composition due to changes in temperature. Plain fraud should not be overlooked, but neither should the beliefs of millions of Christians if a miraculous origin is to be suggested.

'The local priest ... reported that an invalid woman could walk freely after praying to the statue'

Dodleston Poltergeist

Ken Webster's book *The Vertical Plane* provides full details of this outbreak of poltergeist activity in 1984 at a cottage in Dodleston, Cheshire, England, during its renovation. The photos here, taken in May 1985, show what can happen to furniture when such an outbreak occurs. Mr Webster drew attention to a saucepan handle, shown in the shot, that later straightened itself. He also claimed to be receiving messages via paper that had previously been blank, chalk marks on the floor and even his computer. The originator was said to be one Tomas Harden, who lived in the cottage in the mid-sixteenth century.

The problem with these cases is one of belief. Do we believe that everything happened as documented or might it have been done fraudulently for any one of a number of reasons, including mischief, mental disease or financial gain? When the phenomenon has been witnessed by several different people independently it carries far more persuasion. As I mentioned earlier, I can assure the reader that my sceptical views about poltergeists changed dramatically once I had seen one in action.

'The originator was said to be one Tomas Harden, who lived in the cottage in the mid-sixteenth century'

Mind Over Matter

Mademoiselle Stanislawa Tomczyk, a Polish medium, was the subject of a number of experiments in the early twentieth century by such eminent scientists as Theodor Flournoy, Julien Ochorowicz and Baron Schrenck Notzing. Here she is shown allegedly levitating a pair of scissors. These tests took place under strictly controlled conditions, with up to ten cameras being used simultaneously in an effort to detect any fraudulent activity; the findings were published in Schrenck Notzing's *Physikalische Phenomene des Mediumismus* in Munich in 1920. When in trance Mademoiselle Tomczyk claimed to be controlled by a spirit entity called 'Little Stasia' and could produce various movements in objects without physical contact but allegedly through 'rays' that were exuded from her fingertips. Sceptics claimed that she used a very thin thread between her fingers to direct these movements, a technique that can be replicated by stage magicians as demonstrated in the modern colour photo shown here. However, the fact that a professional entertainer can reproduce the effects does not necessarily mean that Mademoiselle Tomczyk and people like her were using sleight of hand. Similar accusations against modern psychics such as Uri Geller, notably one by well-known sceptic and debunker, James Randi, have led to expensive court cases for libel. We are left with the perplexing question of whether someone who is not a professional magician could produce such phenomena under laboratory conditions. If there is reason to believe that they could, then it would be vital for one or more stage magicians to be present at the experiment to help detect the deceit. The colour image shown here, taken in 2003, is an example of a woman emulating Tomczyk around a century after the original, demonstrating how the mystery and debate continue on into the twenty-first century.

'Mademoiselle Tomczyk claimed to be controlled by a spirit entity called "Little Stasia"'

The Stigmatist

In 1951 Antonio Ruffini beheld an apparition of the Virgin Mary and received the wounds of Christ right the way through his hands and feet. These photographs were taken in 1987 and clearly show the scars more than 35 years later. Despite having these wounds for many years Mr Ruffini's hands have not become infected. He celebrated – if that is the right word – this event by having a chapel built on the site of the apparition, to the south of Rome.

There are many questions that might be posed here. Were these wounds self-imposed either fully consciously or in some altered, perhaps divine, state of consciousness? Might they have appeared after deep meditation and then been maintained by some gruesome self-infliction? It is well known that the body will react physically to external psychological or emotional pressures – blushing is a simple example. Many people will believe that Mr Ruffini was indeed blessed by receiving these marks as a sign from God and many stigmatists throughout the centuries have displayed similar signs. The highly contentious and grisly issue of Roman crucifixion techniques might also be considered: although Renaissance paintings show Christ crucified with nails through his hands and feet, it is often maintained that the nails would have to be hammered through the wrists and heels in order to maintain the body on a vertical plane… unless it was tied to the cross first. But stigmatists do not display the wounds of Christ in these places. This is indeed a difficult and disturbing subject.

BACK FROM THE DEAD

I decided to exclude from this book the many possible spiritualistic photographs, some of which were displayed in *Ghosts Caught on Film*, since so many have later been discovered to be fraudulent. Instead, the title of this chapter implies the thorny issue of the survival of the spirit or soul after bodily death, an issue that is always hotly debated – and surely rightly so. The belief systems of various religions provide answers to this question and atheism deals with it easily by refusing to believe in it. But it remains a problem for the agnostics or 'don't knows' who must continue to thrash it around in their minds. I think it is useful to acquire as much evidence as possible in order to try to make sense of the issue. It must be comfortable to be convinced.

Therefore, depending on your point of view, the photographs in this final chapter will either challenge your religious beliefs, confirm your opinion of the gullibility of humans or continue to confuse and intrigue you. As in earlier chapters, frustratingly little information has been made available for some of the images, while others have covering letters detailing the circumstances in which they were taken. Often people have requested no publicity and wanted false names to be used in any filed documentation. In short they are worried that their friends or family will think them cranks or, in some cases, possessed. Photographs of this nature are sometimes sent to organizations like the Society for Psychical Research, many years after they were taken, because the strange appearances were not noticed on the initial superficial glance after development. A common approach is 'Please can you tell us what on earth that object/figure/face/blob/whatever is, since it was certainly not there when we took the photos.' In an ideal world the whole strip of negatives is enclosed: photographic experts can then scrutinize them for signs of tampering or other malfunctions.

My database from which I selected the contents of this final chapter has more interesting photos than any other section, far more than I have space to include. If one adds to these the photographic archives of the groups that have studied this work for, in some cases, well over a hundred years and then considers all the web pages devoted to the subject, there certainly seems to be evidence that something strange is going on here. After my previous book was published I received further information about some of the images in it, and I hope that this happens with this book too, especially concerning this chapter. I believe that we should all continue to explore this most important of undiscovered realms, namely what happens after physical death? Perhaps there is some evidence of tangible survival on the next few pages...

Grandfather Returns

This photograph was taken using a Polaroid camera in Magothy Beach, Maryland, USA, in 1985 – another of the interesting pictures posted on ghoststudy.com. The photographer explains:

We were taking a picture of my grandmother's house, and when the picture was taken… there was nobody in the picture. When the film started showing a picture, you could see an image of what appears to be a person walking up towards the house. My grandfather had just died about three months prior to this photo being taken… and in the photo the figure appears to be walking with his head bent down. This is how my grandfather would often walk.

For several reasons this is an interesting shot. Polaroid cameras do not have a negative and so it is difficult to tamper with pictures. There does appear to be someone in the shot, albeit somewhat blurred, and, according to one commentator, they seem not to be wearing any clothes. Very intriguing.

'My grandfather had just died about three months prior to this photo being taken'

Uninvited Wedding Guest

There are many images of this kind to be found on the internet and in magazines, and one must be very wary of the possibilities of reflection, paintings or people inside the buildings shown. This shot shows Anthony Miller and his daughter Joanne outside their house in Thornaby, Teesside, England, just before Joanne's wedding. Looking at it later Joanne noticed an unknown face in the window – to the surprise of everyone who had been there, since there had been no one else either inside or outside the house at the time. They had the print tested and were told that it had not been tampered with in any way, but the negative was not available since the photographer could not be traced. According to a local writer, Dean Wilkinson, the area had been used as an airfield during the Second World War and at one point had been bombed with a serious loss of life. Perhaps the face belonged to the ghost of a woman who had been killed then and was returning to the area, despite the fact that the house had been built 40 years after her death. Perhaps it was indeed a reflection from outside. Perhaps the missing negative was tampered with. We must decide for ourselves.

'there had been no one else either inside or outside the house at the time'

Highway Man

'could it just be a discolouration in the grass on the bank?'

Eric Spottke believes that the figure on the grass bank on the right of this road in Afton, Minnesota, USA, could be the ghost of a highway maintenance man killed in the area by a drunk driver. This would make it the scene of a violent or unnatural death which seems to accompany so many ghost stories. It certainly doesn't look like an innocent passer-by, the whitish blurred outline giving a definite other-worldly appearance to the figure, but could it just be a discolouration in the grass on the bank?

Roadside puzzles are more common than one might think and in England the phenomenon of hitchhikers who are picked up and subsequently vanish has been reported on many occasions. The area known as Blue Bell Hill in Kent was the scene of several mysterious appearances in 1992, when three different motorists at different times described what they believed to have been a motor accident involving a girl who had disappeared when they stopped their vehicles to help.

Graveyard Child

The story behind this photograph is tantalizing and frustratingly has little provenance other than reports on the website ghoststoriesandpictures.com. Despite its being a well-known and celebrated 'ghost photo', neither the identity of the graveyard nor that of the participants in the mystery are known. It appears that a 17-year-old Australian girl died in 1945 and her mother took this picture on a visit to her grave two years later. She was shocked to find that the photo included the image of a baby or child. She had no idea as to how she had managed to take such a picture or the identity of the child. As far as she could recall there hadn't been anyone else around the grave at the time. In 1990 a so-called 'paranormal expert' visited the area and found the graves of two babies next to the grave of the daughter. Without further details the story and picture have to remain anecdotal, but despite this it is not without points for discussion.

Double exposure is the most likely cause, although one would think that if such a simple explanation was likely, the photograph would never have achieved the notoriety it has. If the story is fraudulent then the only obvious explanation is that it was a somewhat distasteful prank. Death is difficult enough for most people to deal with, especially when a child is involved, so the appearance of the baby is a potent image that could lead to philosophizing on a number of matters embracing both religious and atheist viewpoints.

'the appearance of the baby is a potent image'

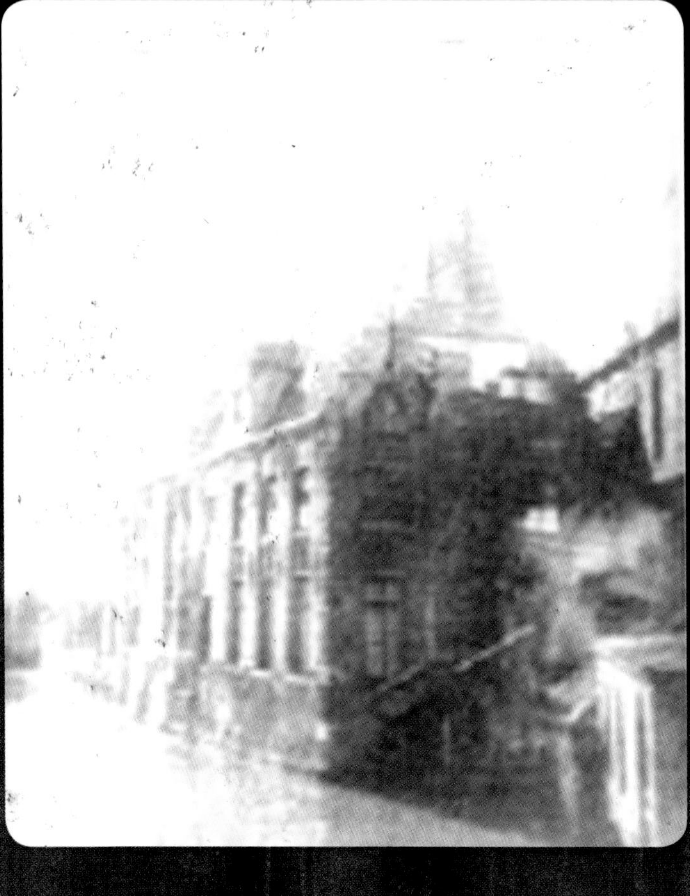

The Bruges Face

Researchers from the television programme *Schofield's Quest* forwarded a copy of this photograph to Maurice Grosse at the Society for Psychical Research after it had been sent to them with a request for clarification. The accompanying letter, dated 14 November 1994, was from a schoolgirl named Victoria from Grimsby in England, who wrote that her father had taken the picture on a school trip to Bruges in 1966. She provided considerable details and opinions as to its source, describing the face as that of a 'beaten-up boy' and the building as 'a gallery for the works of a Belgian artist, Hans Memling'. The photograph had appeared in the *Grimsby News* and had also been studied by the 'London Psychic Research' who asserted that it was a psychic phenomenon. According to the letter the building had been a convent in the thirteenth century and the nuns had found a beaten-up young boy on the steps of the building who they took in and cared for. The boy allegedly later became the celebrated artist Hans Memling.

There are a few problems with this information since Memling was born in Seligemstadt, Germany, between 1430 and 1440 and did not move to Bruges until about 1465 – he died there in 1494. Stories about his life do include his being injured at the Battle of Nancy in 1477 and being looked after by the Hospitallers of Bruges. The photograph could, of course, simply be a double exposure, and without further information it is difficult to form a definite opinion about its authenticity, particularly amid such a muddle of information. Nevertheless, if it is genuinely anomalous, it does seem quite impressive.

'the building
had been a
convent in
the thirteenth
century'

125

Rail Crash Ghost

This is another classic from the archive: a chilling photograph of a serious train crash in Scotland in 1937. Referred to at the time as the 'Castlecary Rail Disaster', it occurred between Glasgow and Edinburgh and was reported in the Glasgow *Daily Record*. The picture, which had accompanied the original report, was reissued in 1966 and appears to show a ghostly figure at one of the carriage doors. It is easy to dismiss it as a doll that has been propped up against the derailed train, but I think that idea needs questioning. Who would perpetrate a practical joke at the scene of such a disaster, especially considering that only the police, fire and ambulance services would have had access to the area? If the 'doll' was stood there to be identified by its owner at a later stage, why did this not happen after the photo was shown in the newspaper? What happened to the 'doll', which no one seems to have found after the area was cleared? Questions, questions with so few answers, which is all too common when one is investigating alleged paranormal phenomena.

'a ghostly figure at one of the carriage doors'

The Birthday Girl

This photograph was one of several taken on 24 June 1982 at a little
girl's birthday party at her home in Coventry, Warwickshire, England.
The photographer's father sent a letter of inquiry with further details:

*When the developed film was collected it was found to have an additional image for which all
reasonable explanations so far have eluded us. The garden is entirely fenced in by a six-foot fence
with little or no chance of either dogs or intruders gaining entry without being observed.*

The little girl seems to be aware of an elderly female figure whose face can
be seen at the window. This could be a trick of the light showing some kind
of reflection from inside, since the face is rather distorted. However, another
photograph from the same film (in the Society for Psychical Research archives)
does not show any such reflection. A medium who was given the photograph to
'read' for psychic phenomena felt there was a definite departed presence, 'unless
Nanny was having a peep to see what she was doing'. Whether the face belongs
to a living or dead relative is for the viewer to decide, but it seems unlikely that an
unknown character managed to be photographed without anyone either realizing
it or knowing who she was. It also seems unlikely that the family would bother
to lie about the circumstances, since there was no prospect of either fame or
financial reward. It remains a mystery.

> 'an elderly female
> figure whose face
> can be seen at the
> window'

129

Cabaret of the Departed

On 25 June 1992 the Society for Psychical Research received a letter from a Mrs G Webster of Halifax, West Yorkshire, England. She enclosed the photograph shown as well as its negative and a different photo of her parents, who had both died in the 1980s but were clearly the people in the background here. Mrs Webster wrote that the local chemist and photographic developer could not explain how they had appeared and that the strip of negatives showed the surrounding images to be normal. The photo was eventually sent to Dr Vernon Harrison, a past president of the Royal Photographic Society, who said that he did not think it was a double exposure and that the negative appeared to be 'normal'. He commented that the faces were about 1.7 times too big (presumably in comparison with everything else in the photograph) and that it did not seem probable that glass was being used to cause any reflections in the vicinity. Dr Harrison admitted that the effects could have been achieved using the process of photo-montage, but in this case it 'did not seem to be at all plausible'.

Maurice Grosse of the SPR believed that either the picture showed Mrs Webster's parents in apparitional form or a thought form had somehow been transferred onto the negative. He concluded, 'One thing is for certain, you have a remarkable photograph …' I agree with him.

'her parents … had both died in the 1980s but were clearly the people in the background here'

The Grey Lady

'It has a tradition of being haunted by a person, usually referred to as a "grey lady"'

This picture was captured on the CCTV in the Reading Room of Willard Library, Evansville, Indiana, USA. It dates from July 2004 and is one of many sightings of the ghost caught on the library's webcam. The library is housed in a gothic building dating back to 1885. It has a tradition of being haunted by a person, usually referred to as a 'grey lady', who is seen briefly and then disappears without trace. The library actively promotes this image via its online video cameras, allowing the viewer to ghost-hunt from the comfort of his or her own home. As to the figure regularly spotted in the reading room there are, as always, various interpretations – a lighting anomaly, fraudulent activity or, of course, a ghost.

The Bogeywoman

This impressive photograph of a ghostly lady was taken in 1929 by Robert D Walsh at Fanham Wood Mill, USA, during the renovation of an inner staircase. She appears to be floating and looking towards the floor. Mr Walsh stated that he did not see anything unusual at the time and had taken the picture to help him assess how much timber would be needed for the building work. He did mention that his dog was acting 'different' that day, but did not specify what he meant by 'different'. The photograph came to light again more recently when it was put into the public domain by Mr Walsh's great-granddaughter. However, she related a story about being teased as a young girl by her sister with the threat that 'Sissy Breeze' would find her if she was naughty and said that Sissy was the person shown in the photograph. The addition of the sisters' childhood story of a 'bogeywoman' does not give any more concrete evidence to the photograph but it does add colour and the possibility that there was a tradition of hauntings at the site, or perhaps that the children were aware of a 'presence'.

'She appears to be floating and looking towards the floor'

Ghost of the Rail Crossing

Who or what is the ghostly figure on the left of this photograph? Is it a smudge in film processing or a phantom from beyond the grave? There are very few firm details concerning this allegedly haunted rail crossing in San Antonio, USA, and the spectral photograph taken by Andy and Debi Chesney. Most sources tell of a school bus stalling on the railway line and a train smashing into it and killing many of the passengers in the 1930s or 1940s. Unfortunately there appears to be no documentation of this tragedy; people seem to know of it only second-hand, as a ghost story. It has been reported that vehicles that stop near the train lines are pushed across the tracks to safety by unseen hands and furthermore that these hands belong to the spirits of the children killed there. Numerous tests have shown that vehicles do appear to roll over the tracks of their own volition and seemingly against the incline. This is not as unusual as one might expect: according to *Fortean Times* (December 2003), many other locations reproduce this anomaly. In tests where talcum powder has been sprinkled over vehicles to discover possible hand and finger prints, small, childlike prints have been produced. One particularly interested reporter, Brenda Pacheco, also heard children's voices and experienced droplets of blood materializing in her car at San Antonio. On the sceptical side, it has been claimed that, despite its appearance, the road has a downward incline towards the tracks and that the prints (from living children) could already have been on the vehicles concerned. Another possibility is that the horrendous bus crash that is known to have occurred in similar circumstances in Salt Lake City in 1938 may have been confused over the years and located in San Antonio by mistake.

'Numerous tests have shown that vehicles do appear to roll over the tracks of their own volition'

Figures in the Back Yard

What we are looking at here is not the bright point of light, which is the reflection of the photographic flash, but the figure to its left at the top of the garden. It was taken by an 80-year-old lady in Mount Juliet, Tennessee, who had apparently long claimed that there were ghosts who regularly visited her back yard. They would walk around for some time and then disappear. Not surprisingly she found that no one believed her and so she decided to take a photograph and prove it. Usually in such cases the photograph doesn't come out or the ghosts mysteriously stop visiting but, lo and behold, back they came and she took this picture. Her relative confirmed that it could not have been a reflection and that the old lady, who had difficulty walking, would hardly have been able to perpetrate such a hoax and she had no reason to do so anyway. The image was posted on the website ghoststudy.com by a researcher affiliated to the Alabama Foundation for Paranormal Research who claims to have visited the site and confirms that 'there really isn't anything that could have caused this by any explained reasoning'.

'there were ghosts who regularly visited her back yard'

Index

Acknowledgments

This book is dedicated to two Lynnes, one formerly Manners and one formerly Nethersole, wherever they are.

Many of the people who affected me before and during the writing of this book are no longer in the physical realm, but I must thank Maurice Grosse, Bob Morris, John Mitchell and Donald Riddell nonetheless. Very much in the domain of the living are Karen Patel, Steve Hulford and my editor Neil Baber, who have all been very helpful. I have continued to receive inspiration from the music of John Kirkpatrick and Loreena McKennitt as I worked late into the night and I could not have undertaken this task without the help and resources of the Society for Psychical Research in London and Cambridge. Finally, I thank you reader for buying this, my latest book. Please remember it has numerous useful purposes ranging from a door stop to an extremely effective guitar foot stall if you buy enough and pile them up (hint) and you might even consider it as a suitable present for friends (or enemies) at appropriate times of the year excluding Guy Fawkes Night when the temptation to use it as a fire lighter may be too great! At Christmas it would be perfect as a stocking filler (for people with strange shaped legs if you ask me) and a birthday present for the person that has everything, since the chances are he/she won't have this tome. Furthermore, you might buy a spare for yourself in case the first copy gets borrowed, bursts into flames, disintegrates or gets eaten by the dog. Thank you.

Picture Credits

These images have come from many sources and acknowledgment has been made wherever possible. If images have been used without due credit or acknowledgment, through no fault of our own, apologies are offered. If notified, the publisher will be pleased to rectify any errors or omissions in future editions.

Front cover, 40 John P/ghoststudy.com; 12 Mike Mellish/ghoststudy.com; 15 Jonap Prasetya/ghoststud. com; 29 Katherine Barts/ghoststudy.com; 40, 69, 85, 133 unknown/ghoststudy.com; 17, 18, 21, 23, 26, 32, 34, 61, 75, 94, 98, 124, 127, 128, 131, Society for Psychical Research; 24 Andrew Green (© Norah Green); 31, 56, 111 hauntedbritain.net; 43 © Fortean/Gruber/TopFoto; 44 © Fortean/Coxon/TopFoto; 46 D Belvins/angelsghosts.com; 49 © Fortean/Adams/ghoststudy.com; 51 Scott Monroe/ghoststudy.com; 53, 54, 72, 80, 83, 89, 103, 104 (b), 109 (both), 118, 122 Fortean Times; 58, 77, 78, 113 (both) © Fortean/TopFoto; 63 © Mason's News Service/Rex Features; 67 © Jamie Jones/Rex Features; 70 (both), 90 (r) © NASA; 87 © Jeff Haynes/AFP/Getty Images; 90 (l) © NASA/Ford/Illingworth Clampin/Hartig/ACS Science Team; 97, 104 (t) © Topham Picturepoint; 100, 104 (b) © AP/TopFoto; 106 © Reuters/Jorge Silver; 106 (b) © Jonathan Wood/Getty Images; 111 (t) © Mary Evans Picture Library; (b) © Charles Walker/TopFoto 117 Jennifer Harvilak/ghoststudy.com; 134 Harp Publications, 137 unknown 138 Blake Wilie/ghoststudy.com